ENOCH POWELL ON 1992

ENOCH POWELL ON 1992

Edited by Richard Ritchie

ANAYA PUBLISHERS LTD
LONDON

First published in Great Britain in 1989
by Anaya Publishers Ltd, 49 Neal Street, London WC2H 9PJ

ACKNOWLEDGEMENTS

The publishers are grateful to the following for permission to reproduce copyright material:

Daily Telegraph, The Field, Hansard, Independent, Management Today, Spectator, Sunday Express.

British Library Cataloguing in Publication Data
A CIP catalogue record for this book is available from the British Library.

ISBN 1–85470–008–1

Typeset by Keyspools, Golborne, Warrington.
Printed and bound in Great Britain by Redwood Burn, Trowbridge, Wiltshire

CONTENTS

But we have our own dream and our own task. We are with Europe, but not of it. We are linked, but not combined. We are interested and associated, but not absorbed.

And should European statesmen address us in the words which were used of old – 'Shall I speak for thee to the King or the Captain of the Host?' – we should reply with the Shunamite woman: 'Nay, sir, for we dwell among our own people.'

SIR WINSTON CHURCHILL

PREFACE

Contrary to appearances, this is not a book about Powell. There have been books about Powell before and probably will be again; but this is not one of them. It is about a decision that the people of the United Kingdom have still to take about who and what they are and intend to be. They have hedged and havered – or permitted their spokesmen to hedge and haver – over that decision for almost twenty years, while all the time it became more and more pre-empted and taken for granted and all the time contradictory and confusing messages were transmitted to the outside world.

It is a characteristic of the British people, not perhaps unconnected with their insular immunity from interference and consequent sense of detachment, that they decline or defer crucial decisions about themselves beyond what to others would look like the Point of No Return. Hitherto, they have always, if I may be allowed a vulgarism, 'caught themselves on' in the nick of time, though not soon enough to avoid high costs internally and externally in material terms and in terms of tarnished honour and reputation. There may indeed be hidden in all this an ancient and instinctive wisdom – the wisdom of the Hythe musketry instructor who advised his pupils not to fire 'until you see the whites of his eyes'. That is no doubt good advice; but it is also necessary to fire when you do 'see the whites of his eyes'.

That Britain had committed itself unawares and was being progressively drawn into a political union of continental nations where it would be extinguished as a distinct, self-governing nation – I abstain from the emotive adjective 'free', though others might prefer to use it for simplicity – was capable, though diminishingly, of being treated as a debatable proposition, as each year passed after the passage by Parliament of the European Communities Act in 1972.

It is no coincidence or accident that for the first time since 1972 the leader of one of Britain's political parties declared in 1988 that the parliamentary self-government of the United Kingdom, no less, is actually at issue, and so opened the prospect that the question will for the first time be given to the electors to answer in the only form known to our constitution – the preference of one party as against another at a general election.

This may help to explain why it is now that Mr Ritchie has made out of Powell speeches the framework of a book about 1992. Thrice at general elections I endeavoured, so far as in me lay, to secure a national verdict upon Britain's future independence as a self-governing parliamentary democracy. The first attempt, in 1970, was premature in so far as at that time the only proposition before the electorate was Mr Heath's famous commitment 'to negotiate, no less, *no more*'. At the two elections of 1974, when the European Communities Act 1972 had already been passed (by eight votes!), the electorate was cheated of its decision because a Labour government reneged upon the plain meaning of that party's election manifesto. With a pertinacity which may have been less than endearing, but which I cannot regret, I nevertheless continued thereafter, whenever I could make myself heard inside or outside Parliament, to expose, throughout all the ins and outs and twists and turns of developments in the Community, in Europe and in the wider world, the underlying question – to be or not to be – which the British people were leaving open. It is for that reason that the story of those last fifteen years and the nature of the arguments and counter-arguments can be deployed now, on the eve of 1992, through the re-evocation of past words of mine.

That Europe – and not only Western Europe – ought, if possible, to be a 'single market' whose inhabitants are not hindered or penalized for exchanging with one another their goods and services (including buying shares in the means of production), is a proposition which probably most people in Britain would now willingly accept. During the last ten years a British government has, with great courage and determination and with manifestly beneficial consequences, insisted that British industry and commerce shall face, and will gain by facing, unimpeded competition from outside. It is indeed a belief which I personally have always shared and commended. There is no joy in paying more for goods and services than we can obtain them for by way of exchange.

What that single market does *not* involve, so far as most people in Britain would agree, is the refusal of a free market in Britain to the Third World or to countries outside Western Europe. A tight protective customs union is not freedom of trade and competition; it is a restriction of trade and a prevention of competition. What is more, a single market does not imply that we have to impose the same laws, policies, and forms of government as our own upon those with whom we trade. The political integration of Western Europe and the creation of political union there have nothing to do with a European single market – or with any free market anywhere, for that matter. It is a bid to create a single centralized political power.

That is the identical point made by the Prime Minister, when in her address at Bruges on 20 September 1988 she declared that 'we have not successfully rolled back the frontiers of the state in Britain, only to see them reimposed at a European level, with a European super-state exercising a new dominance from Brussels'. Those words expose the ambiguity which surrounds 1992 and the European single market and set before Britain and before the rest of the European Community what is for the United Kingdom the be-or-not-to-be question with a starkness and precision that have not marked it for many years. They propound the question upon which the Government will be seeking the British people's decision in the interval before 1992 is reached.

At the consultative referendum held in 1975 the official and statutorily impartial document of guidance to the electors stated that if the majority vote were – as indeed it was – Yes, 'Britain's continuing membership of the Community will depend upon the continuing assent of Parliament'. Here is the answer to those, and they are many, who do not wish to secure a limited area of free trade at the price of accepting political amalgamation into a new 'super-state' – the Prime Minister's term, not mine – but who ask, 'Surely it is too late now to do anything about this?'

Suppressing the temptation to retort that few were heard in June 1940 wondering if it was 'too late now to do anything about this', the reply is that we, the British Parliament, the British people, have the right now to decide what 1992 and the single European market are to mean. What we have accepted, and what no doubt we will honour, is the commitment to place no impediment upon the exchange of goods and services between British citizens and the citizens of the other member states. What we have the right and the power to refuse is to allow that freedom of exchange to be made a pretext for imposing common control upon internal matters and matters of policy affecting more than trade and commercial intercourse. Those matters we intend to retain or (if need be) to get back within the scope of our own decision.

If two or more of the existing states of the Community are minded to enter into political union and amalgamate – if, for instance, the Portuguese and the Spaniards wish to make that experiment again, or the West Germans prefer amalgamation with France and the Low Countries to re-unification with fellow Germans further east – that is a decision for them, in which we would not seek to meddle. What the British people have always wanted to be assured of is their entitlement to live under laws made, taxes imposed, and policies approved by their own representatives in Parliament and by no one else, subject only to undertaking not to use that liberty so as to restrict the freedom of trade between themselves and Western Europe.

This has nothing at all to do with consenting freely to take similar or identical decisions with other nations. It is but rational, when taking some kinds of decisions, to take them to the same effect as other nations. The International Postal Union existed long before the environment was polluted or species were endangered. Our own eyes and ears assure us that on matters of common concern nations – and not necessarily always the same nations – can freely make laws by their own sovereign procedures and binding upon their own citizens, which tend to common advantage. To do this, they need not and therefore do not transfer their own legislative power to an external authority.

The appointment of a specific year, 1992, for the completion of freedom of exchange between the present nations of the European Community has created the opportunity, and, with it, the necessity, for the United Kingdom to put an end to its internal indecisions and its external prevarications. A political issue has now been formulated, which only the people through Parliament are competent to resolve. By happy coincidence the maximum duration of this present Parliament, elected in 1987, expires in the same year, 1992. But something more than a general election is necessary to give the British people the voice to which they are entitled. It is necessary that at least one of the great parties in the state shall be offering them a European single market on the basis of 'co-operation between independent sovereign states' – the expression was chosen by the Prime Minister in her address at Bruges, a state document of Her Majesty's government, and as such neither lightly conceived nor rashly drawn.

Treaties are treaties, and are followed by other treaties. Acts of Parliament are Acts of Parliament, and are amended or discarded by other Acts of Parliament. The abiding reality is the character of the people. By that alone the words of its politicians can be turned into facts.

It is often alleged wrongly that the old are impatient. The error owes something perhaps to that ancient jibe against Gladstone of being 'an old man in a hurry'. The truth is that time teaches patience, a lesson reinforced by the heightened consciousness of being personally powerless. The patience to await something happening which one would have discounted in advance as inconceivable arises from what can only be described as 'faith'. I would call it 'blind faith', if the addition of the adjective 'blind' to the noun 'faith' were not essentially tautological. The faith that somehow – even in one's own lifetime – things will 'come right again' is not wholly irrational. In every natural living thing, and a human society is a complex living thing, there is an inborn or inbuilt principle that makes for its survival. It finds ways of re-asserting its real nature, even in the most adverse of circumstances and even after long periods when that nature has been in abeyance.

If the nation into which I was born is what I believe it to be, nothing can prevent it from sooner or later re-asserting itself. I was wrong when I despaired of this in 1938. I will not make the same mistake at the end of my life as I made at the beginning.

It has not been given to me in any formal sense to represent my fellow countrymen. What was not denied me was the opportunity and the ability to raise my voice in their hearing. Perhaps thereby I became some small part of the means by which eventually they will find their way back to their own true and unique identity as a nation both European and insular, a nation which finds justice and righteousness towards others and towards itself in the institutions of its self-government. Such it has been in the past. Such it will surely be again in the future.

J. ENOCH POWELL

CHAPTER ONE

'FIGHT BACK'

Those who seek to make the United Kingdom a member of the European Economic Community are not speaking for the people of Britain

ENOCH POWELL

'If I were young, I should despair; but I do not.' With these words, on 6 June 1975, Enoch Powell greeted the result of the referendum which had been held the day before to decide whether or not the United Kingdom should remain a member of the European Economic Community.

Many had hoped and expected that this unprecedented constitutional event – as unprecedented as the United Kingdom's accession to the European Treaties – would mark the end of the EEC debate. Despite the many explanations that have been given since, there is no doubt that the result in favour of continuing membership – by a majority of just over two to one – was interpreted at the time, and with some justification, as a massive defeat for those who had campaigned against Britain's membership.

Powell had taken care to distance himself in advance from the débâcle. Before the campaign had even begun, and before it became obvious that the result would be a defeat for opponents of entry, he had said that the referendum 'will not decide whether Britain is to be part of the Common Market or not. What it will decide is whether Britain ceases to be part of the Common Market now or somewhat later.'

It was fortunate for Powell that he offered this opinion. There is no doubt that he believed it. But it did not entirely solve the problem of reconciling the referendum result with his judgment of the national mood only a few years before. In June 1971, he had said:

In the last twelve months, like a heavy sleeper roused at last by an insistent alarm bell, the British have woken up and got to their feet. They have rubbed their eyes and cleared their throats and got ready to speak, to give their answer. It is as though, with one accord, they had said to one another: 'This is not a little thing, but a great business: we will decide it – no one else.'

There is something almost uncanny, something which makes the pulse beat a little quicker, in watching a whole nation instinctively cut through and thrust aside details, pretences, trivialities, and go to the heart of the matter. Untutored, uninvited, and indeed unwelcomed, they have insisted upon discerning the one simple, overwhelmingly important question: to be or not to be, to be ourselves or not to be ourselves.

In these last months and weeks a national instinct and resolution has stirred and visibly grown and taken shape and strength, until the onlooker is tempted to think or say: 'Perhaps, after all, they are the same nation which so many times before has risen late, but not too late, to assert itself in the face of the world.' The question which the people of this country will have proposed to them is: will you, or will you not, continue to be governed by the Queen in Parliament? It is no less than that, and they have understood it.   (Doncaster, 19 June 1971)

But had they? And had the question been put in those terms? This was not to be the last time that Powell would detect a growing popular resentment of all that the EEC entailed, only to be disappointed when this failed to materialize in terms of votes. Indeed, perhaps it is only now, after so many years of practical experience of Britain's membership, that the EEC's full implications are beginning to be discussed in the context that Powell has always wished.

Recent events suggest that Britain's relationship with the European Community is undergoing a reappraisal. If so, there may be some value in considering afresh what the debate is, or in Powell's judgment ought to be, about; and how, in particular, 1992 relates to the deeper issues. Powell has had no ministerial responsibility for any part of the period in question. But whether inside or outside Parliament, he occupies a unique position when discussion turns to the rights and ability of the United Kingdom to pursue an independent path. An appreciation of the current debate may be assisted, therefore, by remembering the nature of the controversy as seen through his eyes only a few years ago.

The referendum is a good starting point. In fact, the mere fact that it took place at all was enough to vindicate, in practical terms, Powell's advice to like-minded Conservatives the year before to 'vote Labour'. At least the British people had been given a chance to speak specifically upon the issue. Without Labour's victories in 1974, the opportunity to vote Yes or No would never have arisen.

But a referendum had not been Powell's primary objective. It was no more than a means to an end – the lesser of two evils. It was certainly not a constitutional device of which he approved, and it is clear that it was not his favoured method of reopening the question. He had hoped that a referendum would turn out to be unnecessary.

Powell's reasons for supporting Labour at the two general elections of 1974 could not have been more simply stated than at a public meeting in Birmingham on 23 February: the electors, he said,

> are now, at a general election, provided with a clear, definite and practicable alternative, namely, a fundamental renegotiation directed to regain free access to world food markets and recover or retain the powers of Parliament, a renegotiation to be followed in any event by a specific submission of the outcome to the electorate, a renegotiation protected by an immediate moratorium or stop on all further integration of the UK into the Community. This alternative is offered, as such an alternative must be in our parliamentary democracy, by a political party capable of securing a majority in the House of Commons and sustaining a government.
>
> (Birmingham, 23 February 1974)

It was Powell's hope and belief that the negotiations would fail, thus obviating the need for a referendum. His preferred course was for the government to inform Parliament that the renegotiations had achieved nothing, and that repeal of the European Communities Act of 1972 was an inescapable consequence of this fact. As shall be seen when the position of the Labour party is considered later, this was not such an unlikely prospect. Michael Foot, after all, occupied a crucial position within the new Labour administration. As Powell remembered, it was he who was on record 'declaring that to the recovery of that independence (lost by the very nature of EEC membership) he would devote his remaining years in politics'. James Callaghan – the Labour Foreign Secretary – had been no great enthusiast for Britain's membership either; and Harold Wilson showed every inclination to leave the European Community if it could be shown to be in his party's interests.

But even if this analysis proved unrealistically optimistic – as indeed it did, and not for the first or last time – Powell, at the very worst, did not see how a government embarked upon genuine renegotiations could possibly win enough concessions to justify neutrality, let alone approval, once any referendum campaign began. It was not his expectation in 1974 that opponents of entry would be campaigning in a referendum against the full weight and official advice of the government machine.

Moreover, his experience of the two general elections of 1974 had persuaded him of his ability to swing votes in the final days of a campaign. It is doubtful whether Powell in 1974 really believed that the referendum result would be so strongly in favour of membership once the argument began in earnest.

Events were to prove otherwise. The first setback for opponents of entry came with the realization that Harold Wilson's concept of what constituted a 'fundamental renegotiation' differed from their own. But, more seriously, the argument became enmeshed with mundane political issues. For example, Tony Benn's position within the Labour government preoccupied the media, and it was judged – probably correctly – that his personal standing would be strengthened considerably by a No vote. That was enough for many Conservatives – and Labour voters too – to cast their votes in favour of Britain's continuing membership. In the opinion of many commentators, the referendum was used by the electorate to pass judgment upon the domestic political scene – and upon the state of the Labour party – rather than to express a considered verdict upon the United Kingdom's continuing membership of the European Community.

In this sense, Powell was entitled to argue after the event that the British people 'still have not been able to credit the implications of going into the Common Market. But', he continued, 'they will learn. I am convinced that in this referendum, the vast majority of those voting had no notion that they were saying Yes or No to Britain continuing as a nation at all. Now what will happen is that gradually, and perhaps not so gradually, it will come home to them that their Yes vote to Europe was No to Britain as a nation.'

One of the purposes of this study is to examine, through Powell's own words and speeches, the extent to which this realization has taken place, if at all; and to consider whether the road to 1992 marks a deviation from, or a significant step towards, the type of European Community against which Powell has committed his whole political energies and strength.

But the question must be approached with a historical perspective; and although the referendum is only some fifteen years ago – far too short a time to attempt a proper historic assessment – it is necessary to understand how this event was regarded by Powell if full sense is to be made of what he has said in the succeeding years. Looking back, some may consider it remarkable how quickly the issue of Britain's membership was resurrected after the referendum result; and how even Margaret Thatcher, in her speech in Bruges on 20 September 1988, is now asking the same sort of questions as were asked by the opponents of entry during the referendum itself.

The problem for Powell was that he could not, during the referendum campaign, find a way of pushing these questions centre stage. The British Establishment had, in his view, taken over; and the Establishment had made up its mind that Britain should remain a member of the Community. Despite the presence of many political heavyweights on their side, the opponents of entry were portrayed as extreme figures who threatened the nationwide consensus of what made sound political sense. Discredited politicians – Edward Heath had, after all, already lost two general elections in succession along with the leadership of the Conservative party – were suddenly transformed into national figures above party politics. And party politics were unpopular in 1975.

Of course, if the country had been minded to take the issue of Britain's membership on its own merits, it could have done so. Supporters of entry were only making skilful use of the electorate's reluctance to reopen a question which did not appear greatly to interest them. It was this fact which compounded Powell's disillusionment. He felt he was facing a conspiracy of the 'great and the good'; and it was not the first time he had felt this.

'If referendum day is not September 1939, at any rate it is September 1938.' Those words of Powell were published in *The Times* two days before polling. Reference to September 1938 was, of course, deliberate:

> Twice, in two periods of my life, I have been ashamed of my own country. The first of those periods was between 1934 and 1939, when a mood of supine indolence, of fearfulness, and of wilful self-deception seemed to lie heavy upon Britain. While the rest of Europe saw and understood the end to which events would lead, an end in which the freedom and independence of Britain would be swallowed up, the British people behaved like the victims fascinated by the predator, incredulous or oblivious of danger or

disgrace. It appeared that we were doomed to slither from one shameful surrender to another until it would be too late to turn. I remember in those years being ashamed to show a British pass- port. I remember also the final sense of relief when it turned out that after all Britain would go down fighting, if go down it must.

The second period of shame has run to this day from 1972, when the British people witnessed their most precious posses- sions, national independence and parliamentary freedom, being surrendered by their own House of Commons. It was an act which one of the great parties in the state, with only minority dissent in its ranks, accomplished and defended. It was an act which the British people, even though a large minority, which eventually turned into a majority, disapproved of it, were content, it seemed, to treat with resigned acquiescence and to regard as no more than one political issue among others of equal importance. I would not have believed, if I had not lived to see it, that this nation could so far forget itself. It is cause for shame.   (London, 4 June 1983)

These words demonstrate a significant contrast from the confidence Powell expressed at Doncaster in 1971; and the analogy of the war was not to be forgotten. Only two years later, to a public meeting in Grimsby on 20 May 1977, Powell said: 'I will not say that you need to travel as far in Britain to find someone who voted Yes in the referendum as in Germany to find someone who was a Nazi; but they are becoming fewer, and the number of those who admit that they were wrong is growing.'

What was, and is it, about the EEC that offends Powell so greatly? What was, and is it, that he fears? No sense can be made of his speeches or actions, no sense can be made of his reaction to current developments, unless the full nature of his opposition is understood.

Some of the practical issues currently raised by 1992 are for Powell merely distractions from the central question. Powell has always been clear that, for him, questions on economics and the 'bread and butter' issues of politics are only symptoms, in the context of the Community, of a much wider question.

Take the following remark as an example: 'In discussing or debating any great matter, there is always a temptation to evade the central issue and to concentrate upon what is secondary or consequential' (October 1980). Or: 'My friend Teddy Taylor, bombarding the Prime Minister with financial and economic statistics, is firing a peashooter at a concrete fort'

(April 1985). The issues for Powell go much deeper, as he explained (in French) to an audience in France in 1971:

> Eight years ago, when your President pronounced the funeral oration upon Britain's previous negotiations with the Community, the issue was seen and presented on our side of the Channel as, I do not say economic, I say merely commercial: the substitution of one system of trading preferences for another. It was viewed in the context of a progressive expansion of trading opportunities which had been taking place: the liberalization measures in OECD; the negotiation for a Free Trade Area with the Rome Treaty countries; the proposal of a European Free Trade Area; the 'Kennedy Round'.

A commercial question

Some pedants insisted on actually reading the Treaty of Rome and talking about political unification; but this received scant attention, on the ground that such ideas were typical continental theorizing, remote from practical possibility, and in any case destined to be held in check by British pragmatism, once Britain should be 'inside'.

All the greater was our astonishment when the President's veto seemed to be concerned with Skybolt and Polaris, Americans and Anglo-Saxons. What on earth had that to do with being inside or outside a customs union or with what had seemed to us the only burning issue – Commonwealth preference?

As for myself, I had entered Mr Macmillan's Cabinet only six months before the veto fell: but I am prepared to confess that in those days I used to argue the case, and counter the objections, on purely commercial grounds with the same sort of reasoning as no doubt Richard Cobden deployed when negotiating the Anglo-French Commercial Treaty of 1860. At least in this respect I shared the general mood of the public, which was vastly unmoved either by the negotiation or its failure.

A mistake

Of course we were wrong. Events have proved us wrong. We did not hear or believe or understand what you were saying and doing on the continent. Only somewhere about two or three years ago [1968] with the emerging possibility that a new negotiation might somehow succeed, did the public wake up, rub its eyes, and unstop its ears. What it heard, to be perfectly fair, was very different on both sides of the Channel – but particularly in Britain – from what it had been hearing when it last went to sleep.

This section of the speech was aimed partly at those who criticized Powell for having changed his mind on the issue of Britain's membership since his time in government. More important, it is a useful reminder of how most people at the beginning of the debate supported the EEC primarily on trading grounds and on the dangers of possible exclusion from the continental market.

There are still many in industry today who continue to see the issue principally in this light; and there are some – Margaret Thatcher appears to be one of them – who wish somehow that the Community could be reborn so that once again trading and commercial freedoms come to be regarded as the linchpin of the Community's existence. But, in Powell's view, this is a typical British misconception; as is now widely recognized, and as Powell warned, such an understanding of the Community and its objectives is seen by many as dangerously limited.

The case for British accession is now both economic (in the full sense) and political. The economic argument is not so much the classic Cobdenite case of as large an area as possible for the division of labour – the 'large home market' – but the claim that, if integrated into an economy which is growing at a fast rate, Britain would be dragged, or shocked, or inspired, into growing at a similar rate – anyhow faster than has been its experience recently or (it might be added) for a hundred years and more.

The political case

This economic argument is, however, officially declared to be secondary in importance to the political argument. This claims that Britain can only have 'power' or 'influence' or 'a voice' in the world of the future by being part of what is called 'a united Europe', which will be in the same class as those other unitary great powers, Russia and America. Sometimes this 'power' or 'influence' is given a specifically military content, in terms of self-defence against Russia with less, or eventually no, direct American assistance.

What is undeniable about this modern version of the case for British accession is that it is not only compatible with economic and political unification, but positively requires it: the advantages now held out can only be realized *pari passu* with the progress of unification; and some of them, particularly the military advantages, do not accrue at all until unification is completed.

Public opinion

The realization of all this has produced a marked reaction on the part of the British public. Before, during, and since the general election [of 1970, when the Conservatives were returned to office under the leadership of Edward Heath] the hostility of the electorate to British entry into the Common Market (we still prefer this name for the Community, in an effort to cling to the concept of a customs union) has been sharp, unmistakable, growing and already – even on the admission of protagonists of British accession – preponderant.

The prime motive of the hostility is not economic; it is not the fear either of more intense competition or of higher food prices and consequently higher cost of living, though both these are voiced. The motive is political. It is repugnance or incredulity towards the possibility of being politically integrated with continental Western Europe. In a recent debate in the House of Commons our Minister of Agriculture [James Prior] said: 'If one were to ask the average British person whether he would rather have two shillings in his pocket with our present economic sovereignty or four shillings without it, I have no doubt what answer he would give.'

Neither have I; but it is the opposite answer to that which the Minister meant. The average British person would reply: 'I don't believe I shall get four shillings by giving up my sovereignty; but I wouldn't if I did, because I never have and I never will.'

Three contradictions

Given this widespread resentment, the British government find themselves forced to argue against their own case, by representing steps towards economic and political unification as remote and in any event capable of being slowed up or vetoed by Britain as a member of the Community.

There are, however, three distinct contradictions in this attitude. One is that it involves arguing against the very grounds on which British accession itself is commended. Secondly, it involves asserting a British attitude which is highly suspect at Brussels: it is necessary to stress the constitutional impossibility of one British Parliament binding its successors, and the intention of Britain to act as a brake on unification. Finally, it is little consolation to those opposed to losing national sovereignty to be told that it will only happen later on and that sovereignty will be retained in detail after entry, provided it has been ceded in principle before entry.

Powell then proceeded to the heart of his argument. He could not then have known that the issues he was raising would become fundamental to what today is known as '1992'.

The negotiations in which Britain is engaged at Brussels relate not to the content of the Treaty of Rome and the rules and nature of the Community – these the United Kingdom openly accepts as not being negotiable – but to the duration and stages of the transition by which the United Kingdom would accomplish her accession.

One of the subjects of negotiation is the phasing-in of the British quota of the Community's common budget, which will presently accrue automatically from the yield of certain defined taxes in all the member countries. One of these taxes is the Value Added Tax, a percentage of the yield of which is to be paid into the Community revenues, to be applied by the Community centrally. It follows that there would not only have to be a Value Added Tax in Britain but that it would have to be the same tax, with the same exemptions and the same incidence, as in the other countries.

Now, at present Britain has no Value Added Tax, and the questions whether this new tax should be introduced, how it should be levied, and what should be its scope, would be matters of debate in the country and in Parliament. The essence of parliamentary democracy lies in the power to debate and impose taxation: it is the vital principle of the British House of Commons, from which all other aspects of its sovereignty ultimately derive.

Logic of harmonization

With Britain in the Community, one important element of taxation would be taken automatically, necessarily, and permanently out of the hands of the House of Commons. This is something quite different from an undertaking by Britain to subscribe, for instance, so much to the various agencies of the United Nations: no one in consequence takes out of our hands the decision what taxes to levy and how and on whom.

Here, in microcosm, is the logic of that harmonization which none can deny to be inherent in the nature of the Community. What is true of the Value Added Tax applies, with parity of reasoning, to every other subject of harmonization. Those matters which sovereign parliaments debate and decide must be debated and decided not by the British House of Commons but in some other place, and by some other body, and debated and decided once for the whole Community.

There is no need to resort to theory and speculation to ascertain whether membership of the Community means the loss of national sovereignty; the fact is implicit in the very negotiations themselves as they proceed at Brussels through a mass of seeming detail. The popular instinct in Britain, that this is what it is really about, is right.

So the question, then, is whether or not it should be allowed to happen.

Whether the answer should be yes or no, for accession or against accession, depends on whether the people of Britain will accept the voice of the people of the whole Community as binding upon them – at first in some, then in more, and finally in all of the essential matters of fiscal, social, economic, and political determination.

When I say 'accept', I mean accept heartily and willingly, no less than the people of all parts of the United Kingdom today accept as self-evidently binding upon them the fiscal, social, economic, and political decisions of Her Majesty's government and of the British Parliament, resting upon the electorate of the United Kingdom. In brief, can we be, and *will* we be, one electorate, one constituency, one nation, with you and with the rest of the people of the Community? I do not believe that anybody who knows Britain can doubt that the answer to that question is No.

The British Parliament

It is a fact that the British Parliament and its paramount authority occupies a position in relation to the British nation which no other elective assembly in Europe possesses. Take Parliament out of the history of England and that history itself becomes meaningless. Whole lifetimes of study cannot exhaust the reasons why this fact has come to be, but fact it is, so that the British nation could not imagine itself except with and through its Parliament. Consequently the sovereignty of our Parliament is something other for us than what your assemblies are for you.

What is equally significant, your assemblies, unlike the British Parliament, are the creation of deliberate political acts, and most of recent political acts. The notion that a new sovereign body can be created is therefore as familiar to you as it is repugnant, not to say unimaginable, to us.

Powell continued:

It is often urged in Britain that one need not take too seriously the commitment of the Community to political unity. Because the realization of that commitment (if it is realized at all) will be gradual, it is alleged that there is no objection to taking into membership of the Community a Britain which is not merely neutral but positively hostile towards political unification. By the time unification comes, they say, the British will have grown used to it – in the jargon this is disguised as 'the habit of working together' – and if unification does not come, no harm will have been done.

I totally dissent. It is not for Britain to gauge the sincerity of the Community's member governments and of the public opinion behind them. It is not for us to judge what you ought to want to do, or what it is possible for you to do. What would be as dishonourable as foolish, would be for Britain and her people to allow the Treaty of Rome to be signed on their behalf with mental reservations.

The enterprise of the Community is on so lofty a plane, the commitment of those who join is so solemn, that we dare not enter upon it, and you on your part dare not accept us into it, unless we can do so *ex animo*, with a genuine and hearty intention that in the fullness of time political as well as economic union shall come out of it.

Therefore it is right that you should have no illusions about the true state of mind in Britain and not be misled by that unanimity and show of confidence which all who speak officially are in duty bound to maintain.

Those who seek to make the United Kingdom a member of the European Economic Community are not speaking for the people of Britain.   (Lyons, 12 February 1971)

It might be argued that this is where the referendum proved Powell wrong. But such a conclusion does not survive a careful reading of this speech. Reference to 'shillings' and the novelty of Value Added Tax betray its age — Britain went over to decimal currency on 15 February 1971, three days after Powell delivered his speech, and VAT came into force on 1 April 1973 — but the principles it discusses, and the arguments it advances, are still to be heard in current political debate.

Take, for example, Powell's warning to the Community in the 1970s not to accept Britain as a fellow member without satisfying itself first that there did indeed exist within the United Kingdom 'a genuine and hearty intention that in the fullness of time political as well as economic union shall come out of it'.

Maybe this sentiment is what Jacques Delors, President of the European Commission, also had in mind when, in an interview with Peter Jenkins in the *Independent* on 7 February 1989, he said: 'I respect the prevailing tendency in British politics [Thatcherism] and I understand the internal difficulties of your country.' Maybe this is what Lord Cockfield meant when he said to the *Daily Mail* just before relinquishing his post as one of Britain's European Commissioners: 'Public relations about Europe has a very long way to go, and perhaps more in the UK than most other countries.'

But Powell's prescience has also been demonstrated in matters of detail. For example, Lord Cockfield himself would probably not dissent from the view that 'there would not only have to be a Value Added Tax in Britain but that it would have to be *the same tax, with the same exemptions and the same incidence, as in other countries*' [my italics]. One of the reported reasons for Lord Cockfield losing his job as one of Britain's Commissioners was because he propounded this position so strongly!

This is where 'harmonization' and 1992 become more than just a difference of opinion about economics, and touch instead upon what for Powell is the heart of politics. As Peter Lilley, speaking as Economic Secretary to the Treasury, reminded the House of Commons on 21 June 1988: 'I agree that there is an excessive passion in some quarters of the Community to introduce harmonization measures that are not always necessary ... We deplore such unnecessary changes, but *they are the consequence of our adherence to the Treaty of Rome* [my italics]. Unless my hon. Friend is suggesting that we should resile from the treaty, we must accept those consequences, while arguing with the Commission that it should not pursue too vigorously unnecessary harmonization measures' (*Hansard*, 21 June 1988 c. 970).

This indeed has become one of the key questions surrounding 1992. For some, like Professor Victoria Curzon Price, of the University of Geneva, 1992 is '... a pure exercise in deregulation, the devolution of power to the market and economic federalism. It is perhaps one of the best, most market-oriented blueprints for economic cooperation that has ever been devised' (*Nineteenth Wincott Memorial Lecture*, 20 October 1988).

But there is an alternative view – namely that 1992 could turn out to be the most concrete demonstration yet of all that Powell has said about the objectives and *raison d'être* of the Community.

One of the difficulties for supporters of 'free markets' – it is obviously not a difficulty shared by interventionists! – is that there is much about 1992 that appeals to their libertarian principles. But Powell has taken great pains in recent years to distance himself from those who believe that free economics is the best and only guarantee of individual freedom. That is why, in order to understand the *political* realities behind 1992, it may prove helpful to recall the nature of the debate as it has evolved since the referendum. No aspect of the European Community should be taken in isolation; and in coming to a judgment upon 1992, it is essential to place it in the wider EEC context. Powell is well placed to help in this process.

CHAPTER TWO

ASSEMBLIES AND PARLIAMENTS

'Parliament' is a word of magic and power in this country.

ENOCH POWELL

Prior to the referendum, the Labour party had refused to nominate any of its members to what was then officially known as the European Assembly. The procedure at that time was for each member country's parliament to nominate delegates from among its own ranks to attend the Assembly's sessions in either Luxembourg or Strasbourg. One of the immediate consequences of a Yes vote at the referendum was the reversal of Labour's boycott. On 7 July 1975, Labour party delegates took seats in the European Assembly for the first time.

Otherwise, the referendum result appeared to make no significant difference to Britain's relations with her fellow Community members. If there was any impact at all, it was to be seen at home. Harold Wilson had taken the opportunity of transferring Tony Benn, against his will, from the Department of Industry to Energy. It took only five days from polling day for this to be effected; it meant that Tony Benn was able to preside over the first landing of North Sea oil a week later.

Powell had to wait some two years before detecting 'the glimmer of a doubt, the first faint dawning of comprehension' among the British people of what the European Community was about. And it was, in Powell's opinion, the 'fishing' issue that was responsible. The United Kingdom's seas, he said, 'are no longer our seas. We have no seas. We signed away our right to them in advance when we became part of the European state in 1973.'

What gave rise to this assertion was the extension of the European Community fishery limits to 200 miles, giving Britain's partners every opportunity and incentive to fish her national waters to their maximum extent. The argument was not resolved until agreement was reached upon a Common Fisheries Policy in January 1983.

But even now, this agreement rests upon the allocation of quotas, which have to be negotiated annually. And even though the policy is meant to last for twenty years, the practice of negotiating in mid-December an annual quota block means that fisheries policy, including the United Kingdom's licensing conditions to regulate the crewing and operations of fishing vessels, is still a highly contentious matter between the United Kingdom and the Commission.

The Labour party's spokesman on fisheries, Norman Godman, remarked on one occasion in the House of Commons that 'among fishermen, the common fisheries policy commands the growing disrespect and lack of trust that many of our farmers show towards the common agricultural policy' (*Hansard*, 1 December 1988 c.907). This is but one small example of the extent to which controversy still surrounds matters that were supposed to have been 'settled', and of how EEC agreements may not always be as final or as satisfying as they seemed before the ink was dry. It is when these isolated examples are all taken together that one begins to understand what, in practical terms, a 'loss of sovereignty' can entail.

For Powell, however, such problems are merely symptoms of a much more profound question. He seized upon the fisheries issue in 1977 precisely because it offered a practical example of a diminution in sovereignty: before fuller realization of the implications a 200-mile limit might involve, he argued,

> the very idea of national sovereignty has been widely treated as a joke, and people could be heard saying that they did not care whether Parliament made our laws or not and even thought they might be better off if we were governed from outside. They did not mean it, of course, hardly any of them. They simply could not imagine that such a thing was actually happening or could happen. So they reacted with a giggle or a shrug of the shoulders, and decided not to bother their heads about it.
>
> (Grimsby, 20 May 1977)

But, in Powell's view, it was impossible to understand the full ramifications of the fishing question, and questions like it, without going to the heart of the matter. In accordance with a pattern that has become familiar, the practical question of fishing was also accompanied at that time by the next step towards fulfilment of the EEC's primary political objectives.

Parliament was about to be asked to agree to the holding of direct elections to the European Assembly. The issue provided a fresh opportunity to consider the direction in which the EEC was heading. On this occasion, however, according to Powell, a change of mood was apparent in the country at large; and it was with this in mind that he reopened the EEC debate by attacking the very concept of what was proposed.

> The impending battle in the coming session [the new parliamentary session was due to start on 3 November 1977] to prevent the direct election of representatives from this country to the Assembly of the EEC will be the most significant since the referendum. I would be prepared to go further and say that it will be the most significant since the great parliamentary struggle of 1972, in which the House of Commons by a margin of votes that could be counted on two hands consented to surrender its authority to an external institution and thus to abrogate the political independence and self-government of Britain itself.
>
> If anyone thinks I exaggerate – not that I ever exaggerate – he has only to listen to the alarm and anger being expressed on the continent at the mere idea that the House of Commons might jib at creating a master over it in its own image. They know, and do not conceal their knowledge, that, once provide it with a directly elected Parliament, the permanence of the new West European state will be entrenched and its evolution guaranteed. Denied that asset, they understand that its reversion to a mere manifestation of the 'Europe of Nations' must sooner or later occur. A battle which your enemy thinks will be decisive is a decisive battle.

In which case, it was yet another decisive battle that was to be lost by the opponents of British membership. In June 1979 direct elections were held, during a four day period, to the European Assembly. (The House of Commons did not officially recognize it as a Parliament until 1986.)

Decisive or not, however, the role of the European Parliament is still much debated and is bound up with the Community's decision-making process – something that has itself been drastically revised to cater for

1992. Powell's fundamental opposition to its existence is explained in the same speech:

> Direct elections to the European Assembly are not democracy; they are the opposite of democracy. Direct elections to the European Assembly are not an extension of parliamentary self-government; they are the negation of parliamentary self-government. Direct elections to the European Assembly are not representation of the people; they are the denial of representation.
>
> Something much more is involved here than the simple fact, important though it is, that the elected representatives of the United Kingdom would be in a permanent small minority — a minority that would become smaller still after the addition of elected representatives from Portugal, Spain, and Greece, if the present pantomime goes on. [Greece joined the Community in 1981, and Spain and Portugal in 1986.] The contrast between being a permanent minority in the existing Assembly of delegates from national parliaments and being a permanent minority in a directly elected Assembly is as great as the contrast between light and dark.

The UK in a minority

As long as the Assembly consists of delegates, the ultimate authority remains with the national parliaments and with the national governments as members of the Council of Ministers. A majority vote in the Assembly of delegates has little significance. Once, however, the Assembly is directly elected, that position is totally changed. What appeal can there be beyond the representatives of the peoples, directly elected for that very purpose?

The very fact of direct election implies the validity and binding nature of a majority: this is the meaning of directly elected assemblies the world over. From that moment the Council of Ministers and the national veto — so far as that actually exists — lose their logic; for their authority is then no greater than that of the national, or local, parliaments, whose representative function in respect of European matters has been superseded by that of the directly elected European MPs.

So one effect of direct election must be to put the UK in a

permanent minority in a body designed in its very nature to exercise decisive authority by majority decision.

Powell then proceeded to the kernel of the argument:

> The essence of parliamentary democracy as our constitution en-shrines it is to render the executive and the legislature amenable to the people, through the answerability of each elected represent-ative to his electors and their periodic opportunity to elect someone else. This whole process is dependent upon one indis-pensable ingredient. That ingredient is party – party programme, party membership, party whip, party government.

He went on:

> Consider the electorate of one of the 81 constituencies which are proposed. I will not labour the absurdity of constituencies averag-ing half a million electors, nor the patronage and skulduggery which would attend upon the assignment of domestic political labels – Conservative, Labour, Liberal, etc. – to the respective can-didates. But they would be elected not because they promised to take the whip of a right-wing, Christian Democrat, or what-have-you? grouping in the European Assembly, nor because of the contents of its manifesto (if it had one), nor contrariwise because of ditto for a left-wing European Socialist bloc. In fact they would probably spend much of their time disclaiming responsibility for any such document or dissociating themselves from any such out-landish companions.
>
> No, they would be elected – either straightforwardly by simple majority or crazily by proportional representation – as a result of the composition in terms of UK politics of the electorate in their particular slab of Britain.
>
> What happens then when majorities in the directly elected European Assembly take decisions, or approve policies, or vote budgets which are regarded by the British electorate or by the electorate of some of the mammoth constituencies as highly offensive and prejudicial to their interests? What do the European MPs say to their constituents? They say: 'Don't blame me; I had no say, nor did I and my Labour (or Conservative) colleagues, have any say in the framing of these policies.' He will then either

add: 'Anyhow, I voted against'; or alternatively he will add: 'And don't misunderstand if I voted for this along with my German, French, and Italian pals, because if I don't help to roll their logs, I shall never get them to roll any of mine.'

What these pseudo-MPs will not be able to say is what any MP in a democracy must be able to say, namely, either 'I voted against this, and if the majority of my party are elected next time, we will put it right', or alternatively 'I supported this because it is part of the policy and programme for which a majority in this constituency and in the country voted at the last election and which we shall be proud to defend at the next election.'

Direct elections to the European Assembly, so far from introducing democracy and democratic control, will strengthen the arbitrary and bureaucratic nature of the Community by giving a fallacious garb of elective authority to the exercise of supranational powers by institutions and persons who are – in the literal, not the abusive, sense of the word – irresponsible.

(Brighton, 24 October 1977)

Powell's views, along with the powers of the European Parliament, have evolved with the passage of time. In 1978 he was of the opinion that:

By participating in the act of electing representatives to the European Assembly the elector, so far as in him lies, expressly withdraws his sanction from Parliament in all matters within the large and potentially unlimited scope of the European Economic Community, and asserts the division of his loyalty as between Britain and an external authority and the superior claim of that external authority in case of concurrence or conflict.

(Co. Down, 5 May 1978)

But a year later, again in Ulster, he said:

There is a great danger that on 7 June those who are opposed to Britain's membership of the European Economic Community – and that is now a clear majority of the British people – will stay away from the polling-booth. The reaction is perhaps understandable; but it is a mistaken one. Boycott is never a satisfactory form of electoral self-expression. (Co. Down, June 1979)

It would be difficult for an official spokesman of a political party – as Powell then was of the Official Ulster Unionists – to say anything different, come an actual election; although it is debatable whether he effectively disposed of the arguments he advanced the year before in favour of abstention.

That has remained a favoured option of many people in the United Kingdom. In the direct elections in 1979, the United Kingdom turnout was a bare 31.8 per cent – although it is worth noting that the turnout in Ulster was much larger, at 55.7 per cent. (Ulster was also unique in being the only part of the United Kingdom where the elections took place on the basis of proportional representation – despite the fact that the House of Commons had repudiated the PR principle for the rest of the United Kingdom, thus preventing the Community from adopting, for the time being, a common electoral system.)

In any case, every election in Ulster is about the Union. In urging people, therefore, to turn out and vote, Powell was no doubt mindful of the Province's political realities where nothing could be allowed to imply a weakening commitment to Ulster's position within the United Kingdom.

In June 1984 the United Kingdom turnout was no better; it was, in fact, again 31.8 per cent – exactly the same as in 1979. But it could equally well be argued that this reflects a general lack of interest in an institution that is still perceived as possessing very little power, rather than a definite intention among opponents of Britain's membership to reduce the legitimacy of the institution by inflicting a derisory turnout.

The Euro-elections in 1989 may turn out to be different – but this chapter must be completed before the campaign has even begun, let alone the results declared. Every indication is that the Conservative party will attempt to win popular support on the basis of Margaret Thatcher's speech at Bruges, in so far as European issues are mentioned at all. It will be interesting to see what effect this may have both upon turnout and the results themselves.

There is also another factor to be considered in the context of elections to the Parliament – perhaps the most important of all. The European Parliament can no longer realistically be dismissed as an institution without power. Powell may have had grounds in February 1982 in London to describe the Assembly as 'a receptacle for failed or superannuated politicians, which provides status, salaries, and a platform for those who could never have got them otherwise.' But even he acknowledged in June 1983, again in London, that the Assembly was a force to be reckoned with:

We are now witnessing the predicted consequences of having accepted a directly elected European Assembly which can hardly be criticized for calling itself a 'parliament', since it possesses the powers that once upon a time made our own Parliament supreme: it can reject the budget and it can dismiss the executive. What more do you need? Its infant and tentative exertion of these powers has already made the Assembly and not the Commission or the Council of Ministers the effective arbiter of the amount of tribute which we pay to the Community and of the terms on which we may have part of it returned to us. Perhaps the bitterest punishment for having so humiliated ourselves is that the very body which the House of Commons made in its own image now wields the lash upon our back.   (London, 4 June 1983)

In December 1982, the European Assembly had rejected the draft supplementary budget that was necessary if the United Kingdom was to receive her budget rebate; in February 1983 a new supplementary budget had been passed, with some of the expenditure in the United Kingdom being charged to 'Specific Community Measures relating to energy strategy'; but in December of the same year, after the date of Powell's speech, the Assembly froze the refunds relating to 1983 that were due to the United Kingdom and West Germany.

There have been further extensions to the European Parliament's power arising from the steps which are being taken towards 1992 and the creation of a single European market. Even before the United Kingdom's adherence to the Single European Act was given in February 1986, the European Parliament had the right to be consulted under some seventeen articles of the Treaty. The Single European Act provides that, for ten of these along with some new ones, the co-operation procedure is altered.

The Parliament now has the power to amend proposals that have been submitted to the Council of Ministers by the Commission, and upon which the Council has agreed a common position. If the Commission agrees, in the light of these amendments, to change its proposal, then the Council, if it still wishes to have its way, must proceed by unanimity. As Sir Geoffrey Howe explained to the House of Commons, 'the new procedure could enable the Parliament to play a more active and positive role in Community decision-taking ... Its negative powers are considerable − the House has always acknowledged that − but its positive opportunities have until now been relatively few' (*Hansard*, 23 April 1986 c. 322).

Powell also participated in the truncated debates that the House of Commons held upon this aspect of 1992. The Bill itself was the European Communities (Amendment) Bill; its purpose was to give the force of law to the Single European Act; and this involved an increase in the powers of the European Parliament:

> When in 1978 the House ill-advisedly consented to convert the European Assembly into a directly elected body, it was predicted that a directly elected body, which was already endowed with the power to refuse assent to the budget of the Community and to dismiss the Commission, would soon discover and explore the potential powers which it would exercise, as in past centuries the House has made a similar discovery and exploration. The anxiety which was expressed on that score was strong on both sides of the House. As a result of that, what professed to be a protection was written into the European Assembly Act 1978, which enacted: 'No treaty which provides for any increase in the powers of the Assembly shall be ratified by the United Kingdom unless it has been approved by an Act of Parliament.'
>
> Hon. Members who have looked at clause 3(4) of the Bill will notice that that is precisely what we are invited to do in approving the Bill. We do not need to argue whether the consequences of the Treaty and the Bill are an increase in the powers of the Assembly. The government say that this is so. The government may seek to argue that that increase of the powers of the Assembly is not at the expense of the powers of the Parliament of the United Kingdom. That proposition rests on an important fallacy about the nature of power. There is no vacuum of power unexercised, unavailable, which is ready to be dished out to new occupiers and exercisers.

The present structure

At the moment, the power exists and it is shared between this Parliament and the institutions of the Community in accordance with a particular pattern. If the power of any portion of those institutions is increased, as the government tell the House it is increased in respect of the Assembly, by the Treaty and the Bill, it must follow that the effectiveness and real power – the political power –

of the other elements, the other possessors, is diminished. Whatever is arrogated to the Assembly by the legislation and the Treaty is deducted from what is available to this Parliament and, thus, to the people it represents.

No unoccupied ground or unexplored territory can be colonized by the Assembly without a diminution taking place in the control and powers of this House. We are discussing an actual deduction from the powers of this House so that those powers may be exercised by other bodies over which we do not have anything like the same opportunity of control.

There is a kind of tripod in the institutions of the Community – the Council, the Commission, and what was hitherto called the Assembly. It is only through the Council that this House can assert itself. It is only in the Council that the members of the government who are answerable to this House can assert themselves. Of course, in the last resort, they can only assert themselves in the Council when there is decision by unanimity. [Powell did not point out that the Single European Act also provided for the extension of qualified majority voting in the Council, thereby diminishing still further the answerability of United Kingdom Ministers to the House of Commons.] Whether they decide in the Council by unanimity or otherwise, it is through the Council that this House still exercises a degree of power, on behalf of the United Kingdom, in the institutions of the European Community.

The new proposals

A big shift is created in the relative power of the Council – its relative power in the tripod – by the Treaty and the Bill. That power is transferred and inures to the benefit of the other two elements – the Commission and the Assembly. Anyone who has studied the co-operation procedure, as it is delicately called, will have seen the joint interest that the Commission and the Assembly have in co-operating with one another.

Indeed, an almost corrupt deal has been struck between the Commission and the Assembly – a log-rolling or back-scratching arrangement between the two – whereby, if the Commission proceeds by way of the co-operation process, it can use the added power which has been attributed to the Assembly to strengthen itself and its intentions *vis-à-vis* the Council. Therefore, it is the Commission and the Assembly, jointly, which are given an accretion of power at the expense of the Council and, therefore, at the expense of this House – the Council being the only element which can be directly influenced and ultimately controlled by the Parliament and people of the United Kingdom.

Powell then proceeded to give a further example of the growing powers of the European Parliament, and to discuss the implications of its new name:

> It is useful to look at the effect of Articles 8 and 9 which amend Articles 237 and 238 of the Treaty of Rome. As the Treaty stands, under Article 237 the decision to increase the membership of the Community is dealt with by the Council after the opinion of the Commission has been obtained. The new article which will replace that provides for the key power to be transferred to the Assembly. That can happen only after the assent of the European Parliament is received. The European Parliament is put in the key position in the expansion of the Community which was hitherto exclusively occupied by the Council of Ministers. If hon. Members will look at the consequences of Article 9, amending Article 238 of the Treaty of Rome, they will see exactly the same process being applied to the process of association.
>
> The Parliament is being inserted in the position of ultimate authority and control which was hitherto occupied by the Council. It is another reminder and indication – it may be marginal in its practical effect but is significant – of the triumph of the Assembly, as against the other institutions of the Community, which is represented by this Treaty and the Bill.

Assembly or Parliament?

That brings me to the third topic – nomenclature. It is no small matter for the House of Commons to declare solemnly that the European Assembly is a Parliament and to bless that nomenclature, although it has been popularly used hitherto. 'Parliament' is a word of magic and power in this country. We refer to 'parliamentary sovereignty'. We live under the sovereignty of the Crown in Parliament. Our history and political life would be unintelligible if Parliament were removed from that history. There is no other European nation of which the same could be said. There is no other European nation at the heart of whose identity and history lies its parliamentary assembly.

When we proceed to accord the title 'Parliament' formally and by the law of the United Kingdom to another assembly, we should be conscious of the symbolical nature of the act which we are performing. We are endowing that institution potentially with the same sovereignty, powers, and representative quality that we in this Parliament possess. It is an act of meaning. It is not something that we can dismiss as a mere formality, a matter of nomenclature to be hurried over. It is significant and, if there were any possibility of otherwise mistaking the meaning and importance of the Treaty and the Bill, we should be put upon warning by this part of the legislation.

Finally, Powell returned to a theme he had explored before.

Merely to be elected is not to be democratic, in the sense that we understand it. There is a certain relationship between electorate and elected body upon which the very nature of parliamentary sovereignty and our claim to be a representative body depends.

Our parliament is a homogeneous body. It wills a single nation which elects the disparate Members who sit together in the House. It is the Parliament of a united kingdom. The Parliament which assembles at Strasbourg is an assembly of those who have been elected in different nations, and, incidentally, under different electoral systems, to congregate together. They do not come together as the representatives of a single self-recognizing community. The nature of that assembly is different in kind from the nature of this Parliament.

We are performing a type of solecism in attributing the term 'Parliament' to that Assembly. What we should not do is create implications and hallow assumptions which attach to the word 'Parliament' when applied to the European Assembly. The European Assembly is not, in our sense of the term, a 'Parliament' and it is not the wish of the people of this country that it should ever be a Parliament in the sense of being the ultimate repository of the legislative and executive powers under which the people of the United Kingdom are to live.

By sanctioning these changes, and especially the change in nomenclature, we are perpetrating a lie in the face of Europe, implying that the British people voluntarily intend to surrender to the institutions of the Community those powers over themselves which hitherto have been exclusively vested in the House. They do not intend to do that. When they become aware that that is what is happening, they will put a stop to it.

(*Hansard*, 26 June 1986 c.495–8)

As mentioned above, the extension of the powers of the European Parliament was not the only change to be introduced into the EEC's decision-making process. Of equal importance – if not greater – was the introduction of qualified voting within the Council of Ministers. This now means that it is impossible for a *single* country to block a proposal linked to the single market. In practice, the combined votes of *three* countries are needed to exercise a veto.

In fact, the right of veto is itself a matter of debate. The so-called Luxembourg compromise of January 1966 states: 'Where, in the case of decisions which may be taken by a majority vote on a proposal from the Commission, very important interests of one or more partners are at stake, the Members of the Council will endeavour, within a reasonable time, to reach solutions which can be adopted by all the Members of the Council while respecting their mutual interests and those of the Community, in accordance with Article 2 of the Treaty.'

The effect of this agreement in practice was to extend the unanimity rule over a wide area. Or so it was thought. But on the one occasion when it was formally invoked by the United Kingdom – on 18 May 1982, during the agricultural price-fixing negotiations – it was overruled, with the other members disputing the validity of the assertion that vital national interests were involved. Peter Walker, the Minister of Agriculture at the time, told the House of Commons that the incident 'created a very sad and damaging day in the Community's history'.

As the Foreign Secretary reminded the House of Commons during the passage of the European Communities (Amendment) Bill in 1986, 'the Luxembourg compromise is not a provision of the treaty.' It is still, in the government's view, a weapon to be used 'in the last resort'. But 1992 reduces the number of occasions when it is a practicable option – and in the government's view this is a good thing.

None of this detracts from Powell's fundamental assertion – indeed it strengthens it. The Council of Ministers is the Community institution over which the House of Commons wields most control; anything that diminishes the scope of a British minister effectively to block a proposal weakens also the right of the House of Commons to say 'yes' or 'no'. Inevitably, this opportunity is curtailed by the introduction of qualified majority voting within the Council. Coupled with the new rights of consultation given to the European Parliament, particularly when the Parliament and Commission are united against the Council, the House of Commons increasingly finds itself in a position of diminishing power.

One further thought is relevant to the aspect under discussion. The politics of nationalism are once again beginning to assert themselves in Scotland. But this time independence may be judged more credible than on the previous occasion, when the offer of 'devolution' was seen as a way of fudging the issue. Perhaps this is not so surprising given the fact that the European Parliament, in which an independent Scotland would continue to be represented, enjoys so much greater authority than when Scottish independence was last on the political agenda in any serious manner.

CHAPTER THREE

FREE TRADE, 1992, AND MONEY

There is nothing which comes nearer to sovereignty, self-government or what politics is about than control of money.

ENOCH POWELL

The debate concerning the future powers and role of the European Parliament is a good illustration of the impossibility of divorcing 1992 from the political ramifications that surround it.

In June 1985, Lord Cockfield published his White Paper on completing the European Community's internal market. At the time of writing, some nine-tenths of the White Paper's two hundred and seventy-nine legislative goals are already the subject of legislation or of proposals by the Commission. Nearly one hundred have actually taken the form of legislation. It is inconceivable that such progress could have been made without an acceleration of the Community's decision-making process as described in the previous chapter.

True, some of the most sensitive areas have still to be agreed, and there is still considerable doubt whether the programme as a whole will be completed successfully. But there is little doubt that, without the Single European Act, the Community would have made negligible process in achieving its objective of a 'single market' by the first day of January 1993.

Opponents of entry have thus been proved right; the Community *has* been forced to move towards majority voting with all that that entails for absolute sovereignty. 1992 has been the catalyst. And in the view of all those who support the principles behind 1992 – of whom there are many, including some who are by no means hostile to the economic principles for which Powell has fought during most of his political life – 'a good thing, too'.

It is now necessary, therefore, to consider the measures themselves, and the principles that lie behind the creation of a single market. But it should be noted, in passing, that Powell has already informed the readers of the November 1988 issue of *Management Today* that 'There ain't gonna be no 1992'.

This statement is likely to be added to the long list of Powell predictions that, from his point of view, are born more from optimism than from an objective analysis. They are part of the war of words – and should be taken no more seriously than the assurances of victory that every candidate gives his voters at election time.

That, at any rate, might be an immediate reaction. But it may also be mistaken. The term 1992 embraces a legislative process that has already begun, and that is due to be completed by the first day of 1993. In this sense, the only way 1992 'ain't gonna be' is if Britain leaves the Community in the meantime – or if the Community ceases to exist in its current form.

The second of these may be less fanciful than the first, although only Powell would regard either as likely. Lord Cockfield is fully entitled to claim, as he did in an interview in the *Daily Mail* on 29 December 1988, that 'the momentum to 1992 is now unstoppable', but he also concedes that Britain could choose to remain on the sidelines. The development of a two-tier Europe – although inimical to the protagonists of Britain's EEC membership – is one of the ways that Britain could leave the Community without having to admit that it had done so.

Much also depends, however, upon what is expected of 1992. Sometimes things 'happen' in an entirely different way from what was expected. This is what Powell meant when he said in December 1978, 'Seven years ago [i.e. 1971] – it was in a speech at East Ham – I predicted that Britain would not join the EEC. I was not mistaken. We never have.'

His point was that, despite all that had taken place, Britain had not in reality shown any wish to take membership of the Community seriously and was still attempting to carry on as before. This was not just Powell's view. Four years later, in December 1982, he took comfort from the words of the then President of the European Commission, M. Gaston Thorne: 'The integration of Britain into the EEC has been harder than had ever been imagined.'

Opponents of entry must take care not to press this argument too far, for fear of negating their own case on sovereignty. Much of their argument rests upon the assertion that, in the final analysis, Britain will be forced to comply with laws and taxes over which the House of Commons has had no say. If Britain can be – indeed, already is – a 'sleeping partner', why all the fuss?

Nevertheless, it is in this sense that Powell believes there is room for scepticism so far as the inevitability of 1992 is concerned, particularly among the business community:

> In lieu of endeavouring to anticipate rumoured fiscal and legal changes, let us wait until the changes have become part of British law. Let us not be stampeded by those who threaten us with the fear of being left behind: that was the wisdom of the Gadarene swine. It will be those who act in anticipation of what does *not* happen who will get their fingers burnt.

He continued:

> What would you have said in 1984, had you been told that in 1988 the Cruise missiles would be trundling out of Britain for destruction? What would you have said in 1984 had you been told that in 1988 a British Prime Minister would say that 'the European Community is not the only manifestation of European identity: we shall always look on Warsaw, Prague, and Budapest as great European cities'? Did you really in 1984 look forward to seeing the American President in Moscow and the Soviet General Secretary in Washington?
>
> Unless you can sincerely answer those questions and others like them in the affirmative, let Cromwell, as he once did the Long Parliament, 'beseech you in the bowels of Christ to think it possible you may be mistaken' in your confidence in those who tell you just what it is going to be like in 1992.
>
> (*Management Today*, November 1988)

One reason for taking this warning seriously is because it is now clear that 1992 means different things to different people. There is a clash between those who see it as an instrument for promoting free trade, and those with more far-reaching political and economic objectives. If it should turn out that the British perception of 1992 is entirely different from the view shared throughout the rest of the Community – and that the two positions are irreconcilable – the implications would be far-reaching. That is why the purpose and thinking behind 1992 are so important.

Powell had anticipated the arguments that are commonplace today, long before 1992 had ever been spoken of as a target date for the creation of a single market. For example, in 1979:

> The Community is not about free trade; the Community is about perfect internal competition – which is something essentially different. It is also about common restriction of external trade. There is no such thing as perfect internal competition and common external trade regulation between free nations.
>
> (London, 29 June 1979)

Or again, in 1980:

> The combination in the EEC of the British economy and the continental economy had not extinguished the special characteristics of the British economy – geographical, physical, social, commercial, industrial, and agricultural – but had ensured that they would produce increasing penalties for Britain within the European system. For Britain, that is, as a national economy; but that was not what the rest of the EEC meant, and means, by convergence. For the other members, and for the Community, convergence meant amalgamation, the absorption of hitherto national economies into a new economic state, towards which they would all converge until eventually they were related to it as regions to the whole.
>
> (Milton Keynes, 28 March 1980)

And, finally, Powell has referred to 1992 specifically:

> 'The meaning of that blameless date, which all of us who survive long enough will one day experience, is beginning to come clear. It is not the year of freedom of trade. There is a lot to be said in favour of freedom of trade, of governments not impeding the exchange of goods and services, not to mention currencies, between their own citizens and the inhabitants of other lands. The

EEC however is not, and never has been, about freedom of trade: it is about, and always has been about, a closed-off internal trading system in Europe. What 1992 means to the EEC is something quite different from freedom of trade, something which is based upon a fallacy as monstrous as those discredited absurdities of the early 1970s.

Freedom of trade, the fallacy asserts, cannot exist between countries unless they have the same tax laws, the same currency, the same standards of drinking water and bathing beaches – unless, in short, they are a single political unity.

Now this is the negation of free trade, of the freedom to exchange one's goods and services with the other fellow, however stupid and however different from our own his customs and his laws may be. What the EEC is bent upon has nothing to do with free trade or free anything. It is a naked assertion of the will to power, the will to create a unified state to which instead of our own national organs of representation and government we are all to be subordinated.   (Halifax, 26 September 1988)

And two years before, during Parliament's discussion of the Single European Act, Powell had raised the same issues with specific reference to tax harmonization:

What is quite clear about the harmonization of taxes, whether it is up or whether it is down, is that the resultant system of taxation will not be one which this country has chosen. It will not be a system of taxation which has been proposed to this House or which has been legislated for by this House. It cannot be harmonious and it cannot converge, if that is the case. There is no respect more than this in which the will to political power, by membership of the EEC and the EEC structure, is evident.

The alleged purpose here is the completion of the internal market. If the internal market means freedom of exchange and freedom for the movement of goods, it is quite untrue to say that such freedom is dependent upon the approximation of the various tax systems in the different countries of the Community. All taxes have an economic effect. Therefore, if we want to harmonize the economies of two or more countries, we must enforce harmonized taxation in those countries; but there is no necessary connection between the harmonization of taxation and the freedom of trade, other than that freedom of trade is a pretext and a cover for the will to power and the will to political unification.

(*Hansard*, 10 July 1986 c. 512–513)

'*A pretext and a cover for the will to power and the will to political unification.*' With these words, Powell entered areas of dispute that now, three years later, are at the heart of the debate. The Chancellor of the Exchequer, Nigel Lawson, has also said, for example, that 'enforced tax approximation is in no way a necessary feature of the single market.' But, unlike Powell, he denies that political unification is what 1992 is, or needs to be, about. For him, free trade is the sole and sufficient justification.

The irony is that there are probably many in the EEC who would agree with Powell's interpretation of what is going on, although it would be bad tactics for them to say so openly; but in this country, a different view of 1992 is often taken and Powell's approach is considered, in the words of Sir Geoffrey Howe, 'terrors for children'.

There must, however, be something to be said for the position that Powell, among others, expresses; otherwise why should Lawson and other members of the government take the trouble to emphasize what they claim to be axiomatic? Lawson has said, in an important speech, already quoted above, which he made at Chatham House on 25 January 1989, that 'the United Kingdom is committed to breaking down barriers, *so that the single market really is a free-trade area*' [my italics]. In other words, it could be something else.

Lawson has also asserted that diversity is compatible with a free-trade area: 'Different countries have different approaches and do not see why they should change their ways. The breakthrough of the single market was the acceptance of the principle that there is no reason why these national differences cannot continue, applied to a country's own products and businesses, *provided* each country accepts that firms and products approved in one country should be free to compete throughout the Community and that people should be free to purchase goods and services from anywhere within the Community.'

There would be no need to labour the point if there were no opposite interpretations. What Lawson states may be true of a free-trade area; the question is whether it is true of 1992.

Jacques Delors by implication thinks not. Free-trade areas are not difficult things to create, given the necessary political determination and commitment. They can provoke serious domestic political difficulties, but they do not require elaborate legislation. They are an exercise in negotiation rather than law making.

Perhaps, then, Delors had something else in mind when he confessed that 'My feeling is that we will not be able to take all the decisions which will be necessary from now [July 1988] until 1995 unless there is the embryo of a European government in one form or another ... ten years hence, 80 per cent of our economic legislation, and perhaps even our fiscal and social legislation as well, will be of Community origin.'

And Lord Young appears to think the same. When questioned on a BBC television programme in October last year about 1992 ('On The Record', 9 October 1988), he was asked specifically what proportion of legislation he expected to come through the European Parliament. He replied: 'Well, already there are large areas which are coming through from Europe, it might be a third, it might be a half, it depends on the particular area of legislation.'

If Lawson's concept of a free-trade area is correct, why is so much legislation needed? And why the apparent contradiction between ministers? Powell would answer: because much more than free trade is at stake.

The issue is complicated still further by the fact that discussions about 1992 invariably turn to questions of currency fluctuations and the management of money. For some this should be out of bounds in the 1992 context; but in practice it is impossible to ignore the extent to which the two are related, particularly when the architect of the proposals, Lord Cockfield, has himself said in the interview quoted above: 'The view I have always expressed is that we ought to have a single currency as soon as possible after 1992.'

The debate currently raging upon the monetary framework of the EEC, therefore, may be assisted by reminding ourselves of how it all started.

The first step is to consider the role and purpose of the European Monetary System (EMS), which came into force in March 1979. It had originally been proposed in October 1977, and what distinguished it from past attempts to stabilize currency fluctuations was that it was supported by financial solidarity mechanisms and a common currency unit – the Ecu.

One question that was immediately asked, and has been asked ever since, is whether the EMS is a stepping stone towards full monetary union; or whether it is something entirely different and is, in Lawson's words, merely 'an agreement between independent sovereign states whose economic policies remain distinct and different'.

Powell has never had any doubts. In August 1978, he said that 'Currency alignment, given the free trade which virtually exists in the Community already, *is* economic and monetary union; and economic and monetary union *is* political union, as soon as the blinkers are taken off.'

Or again:

> A common currency means common government: the one is meaningless and impossible without the other. Accept common money and you have accepted common government.
>
> Do I have to spell it out with matchsticks? National currencies do not automatically remain in fixed alignment. If one threatens to diverge, what happens? 'Oh,' say the rules of the game, 'the others will lend it their money with which to bid up the price of its own currency.' And when (as they must) they get tired of lending to it, what then? They order it to alter its ways and dictate to it how to do so.
>
> Who then is going to do the dictating? Where will be that common government which a common currency implies? You guessed it. 'Paris-Bonn accord on European currency' run the headlines. France and Germany, who hatched and willed this business, will see to it that they rule the roost: a Franco-German hegemony to begin with, and afterwards we shall see whether it will be French hegemony, as France intends, or a German hegemony, as the Germans never cease to purpose.
>
> All this has nothing to do with common markets or freedom of trade or all the alleged ideals of the EEC. Quite the reverse. This is not about freedom: it is about compulsion.
>
> (Newbury, 3 October 1978)

That is why he was so overjoyed two months later when Britain 'temporarily' stayed out of the exchange-rate mechanism of the EMS when it was inaugurated in March 1979:

> The decision of Her Majesty's government not to join the fixed system of fixed currency ratios, known as the EMS or European Monetary System, is the beginning of the end for Britain's membership (in anything recognizable as its present form) of the European Economic Community.   (Greenwich, 15 December 1978)

Powell's view of the EMS is in fact often contradicted. Many see it solely in terms of a co-operative effort to reduce currency fluctuations. Even those who see little merit in making such attempts to align currencies do not discern behind them any sinister attempt to introduce monetary union by stealth.

The distinguished economic commentator Samuel Brittan, for example, is very much in favour of linking sterling with the D-Mark via the EMS as a means of fighting inflation. He has spoken of 'the old Keynesian canard' that says that European monetary union requires a common fiscal policy.

Then there is one of the Prime Minister's economic advisers, Professor Sir Alan Walters – who, while disagreeing with Brittan about the economic effects of Britain joining the EMS – nevertheless accepts 'that the half-baked EMS is a long step away from a monetary integration of a United States of Europe' (to which, incidentally, he would not necessarily be opposed).

Or one can turn to Sir Leon Brittan, who discussed this aspect of 1992 on 10 February 1989 in one of his first speeches as a European Commissioner. He believes that both because of 'the realities of exporting' and 'the need for continual vigilance in the battle against inflation', Britain 'would be best served now by fully joining the EMS'.

But like his President, Jacques Delors, he was not satisfied to leave the argument at this point: 'As to developments beyond the EMS, the increasing interdependence between the economies of the different member states is inevitably leading to greater co-ordination of member states' monetary and exchange rate policies.' And he concluded: 'increased monetary co-operation *is* again on the agenda, and it is too important an issue for Britain's voice not to be heard. Only as full members of the EMS can we really hope to influence its future direction.'

If Powell was able to accept Sir Leon's premise, he might find nothing exceptionable in this analysis. But since 1992 encourages Britain's participation in the EMS; and since the EMS is regarded by our EEC partners as a step towards monetary union – then Powell, given his own political objectives, is perfectly justified to be worried by the single market and all that it entails.

He would have further cause for concern given the views of Delors himself who, although he claims to make a significant distinction between closer co-operation within the existing EMS and the hopes of building in ten or twenty years a United States of Europe, nevertheless often seems to link the two.

In a revealing interview with Peter Jenkins in the *Independent* of 7 February 1989, Delors says it is for the achievement of 1992 that he hopes 'that the British government will reconsider its position and allow the pound to join the exchange-rate mechanism of the EMS.' He does not believe an efficient single market can operate without the minimum of co-operation offered by the EMS in the macro-economic and monetary fields. But he professes that economic and monetary *union* is something quite different – different, though not of another world.

'My feeling,' he said, 'is that many chiefs of government will not accept standstill in the Community. That is because for many governments, the final purpose is political union. Political union is not for tomorrow. But without this political purpose it would not be possible to overcome the internal contradictions of Europe and achieve the single market. That is the reality. If governments were to say tomorrow: "Our only goal is to achieve the single market", then it would not be possible to achieve the single market.'

On this reasoning, it seems that 1992 does not mean economic and political union; but it cannot happen unless economic and monetary union is declared to be the final objective. No wonder that Powell – and others of his persuasion – are suspicious.

What is at stake here is a difference between economic and political judgments. Free economists who subscribe to the views of organizations such as the Institute of Economic Affairs will argue, as has Professor Curzon Price, that: 'The EMS is not a nascent European Central Bank, nor the future fountainhead of a single European Currency. It is just a cartel of central banks attempting to anchor their currencies on the wing of a butterfly ... It is not for nothing that the single-market project does *not* include the creation of a single Community currency. However much the business world may yearn for the stability that this would provide, the single market needs the degree of flexibility that occasional currency adjustments provide' (*Nineteenth Wincott Memorial Lecture*).

But do such economists fully understand the world of politics in which Powell has lived his life?

> In this debate we are arguing and eventually voting for or against the principle of monetary union. If I am asked how I know that, my answer is because it says so. By article 20 we are writing into the law and the Treaty
> 'Chapter 1, Co-operation in Economic and Monetary policy (Economic and Monetary Union)'

Note the brackets. It begins:

'In order to ensure the convergence of economic and monetary policies which is necessary'.

There is nothing which comes nearer to sovereignty, self-government, or what politics is about than control of money. From the beginning of time it has been the attribute of sovereigns that they made or declared money. Their image and superscription was found upon it. That is what made it money. In our day, supremely the subject in politics about which we dispute, debate, and vote between elections is about how the control of money shall be exercised and how the state to which we belong shall use the power of the modern state to make, or sometimes to unmake, money.

There are signs that a general election has been discerned on the horizon by the parties in the House. One of the principal issues, if not the principal issue, between the parties which will be put to the electorate is alternative ways in which the British state ought to use the money-making power.

If there is to be monetary union that decision is to be taken away from the British people. It is no longer to be a subject of politics in this country. It is a subject which will be decided by the general and common authorities of a monetary union. Consequently, there is nothing more directly and clearly inimical to the political process in this country than the professed intention to enter into a monetary union.   (*Hansard*, 10 July 1986 c. 526–7)

CHAPTER FOUR

'INEXTRICABLE ATTACHMENT'

*What I do find lacking, and alarmingly lacking, is still any
understanding of what kind of animal the EEC really is.*

ENOCH POWELL

The politics of 1992, however, are not the only aspect of a single market
that Powell criticizes. He is suspicious too of the economic consequences
and in a way that might surprise those who have associated him with un-
adulterated Manchester liberalism.

Certainly he is opposed, as one would expect, to 'Fortress Europe'.
This is well illustrated by a speech he made on the subject of aid and under-
developed countries:

The whole colossal structure of international aid in all its forms is
crypto-imperialist. It is the principal, though not the only, guilt for
which we owe apology to our victims. The ex-Imperial powers set
out to impose economic structures of their own choosing upon the
ex-colonial nations, and they succeeded in doing so virtually un-
checked and unchallenged because they purported not to be doing
it through the exercise of political power. The new nations were to
produce and export what it suited the West for them to produce
and export; they were to invest in what it suited the West for
them to invest.

No doubt this was not purely the result of an unconscious
psychological hangover on our part from the days of European

empire. Self-interest, if not very far-sighted self-interest, was also at work. To be aware of it you need only listen to donor governments, including our own, impressing upon their citizens that aid is a good bargain because it will be spent at home in ways that create employment.

Our old industrial pattern, threatened with disruption if we accepted what the new countries were able to sell to us, could be preserved by giving them sums of money instead with which to meet their trading deficits and incidentally to pile up fantastic mountains of indebtedness.

Aid was the salve with which the West soothed its psychological trauma: it was also the weapon with which the new countries were kept in European economic thrall. The operation worked, because it could count upon the vanity, the self-seeking, or the corruptibility of the new ruling regimes: they could be made willing accomplices of crypto-Imperialism.

The European Community is guiltiest of all. In pursuance of its autarkic policy of European self-sufficiency, it not only excludes or penalizes the cash crops which the rest of the world is willing to offer but it wrecks the alternative markets for those products by offloading the surpluses which its own wealth is strong enough to create.

It is, and always has been, cash crops for export and low-cost manufacturing that are the defence of a less advanced economy against the Nemesis of famine which attends reliance on subsistence agriculture. When the West stands aghast at the destitution of the new countries it is looking upon its own handiwork.

(Rossendale, 25 September 1985)

But Powell's opposition to 'Fortress Europe' does not mean that he ignores national considerations when it comes to foreign ownership of British companies. Such questions are all tied up with 1992, and the role of the Commission. Contentious areas include the powers of individual states to block changes in the ownership of their national companies on grounds other than competition – such as, for example, national security.

An episode that has been long forgotten, but was considered very important at the time, prompted Powell to deliver a speech that is instructive on this aspect of the subject. In the mid-1970s, the plight of Britain's car industry became one of the touchstones of the 'industrial strategy' pursued by the then Labour government. Chrysler (UK) was one of the car firms in greatest difficulties, and after acrimonious debate (within the government) and tough negotiation (with Chrysler itself), the government agreed to contribute substantially to Chrysler's expenditure and to share its financial risks. The alternative was Chrysler's threatened withdrawal from the United Kingdom.

This, in December 1975, was described by the Conservative party at the time as one of the most notorious interventions of Labour's industrial strategy. Two years later the firm was still struggling for survival, and it became clear that the government's rescue package had no chance of success. Another alternative presented itself, however, in 1978:

> The purchase of Chrysler (UK) by Peugeot is a proposition which raises issues of quite exceptional interest and instruction. Not all of these seem to have been canvassed or understood during the period since the Peugeot offer became known. The political implications are the important ones; but it is necessary to get the economic grammar clear first.

Foreign takeovers

When foreigners buy a firm, the purchase price normally represents the equivalent volume of investment from abroad in the country where the firm is situated, but not usually investment in the particular industry of which the firm is part. For example, if some Japanese buy out the shareholders in a plastics firm in Britain, that in no way means that Japanese capital is being invested in the British plastics industry.

What it does mean depends on what the former shareholders will do with the money they get. Only if they use it – which is unlikely – to acquire new capital themselves in the British plastics industry, has investment in that industry been increased. Otherwise, one can say no more than that the capital seeking investment somehow somewhere in Britain has probably been increased to roughly the extent of the purchase money.

By and large, that is no doubt welcome; and for that reason I have never been among those who have feared or resisted the purchase by foreigners of industrial assets in Britain. Wherever the additional capital has gone, it has been added irrevocably to

Britain's stock of productive capital. The foreigners can no more take it away again than we can recover from the streets of Buenos Aires the tramlines laid there with British savings.

Chrysler-Peugeot

This, which I have just painted, is the classic picture of foreign investment through purchase of existing assets. But in the Chrysler-Peugeot case these consequences and benefits accrue not to Britain but to the United States. Unless any Chrysler Corporation shareholders who are British-domiciled decide to repatriate the money they get from Peugeot, what will have happened is that a quantity of French savings will have been added to American investible capital. On Britain there would be no capital economic effect, and no current effect either, as there would be no change in the existing rights to send abroad from Britain any profits made by Chrysler (UK).

For Britain, the effect would not be an economic one, but a political one – the replacement of one set of foreign owners of industrial assets in Britain by another set of foreign owners, or, to be precise, of American owners by French owners. It is the implication of that political change which ought to determine the government's decision whether to give or to withhold the authorization of the sale which is unquestionably and admittedly their right.

Powell turned, therefore, to the political implications:

So HMG are indeed deciding, in the national interest, between American or French ownership of this undertaking. What is the difference, then? The difference is in the relationship between the Chrysler Corporation and the American state on the one hand and that between Peugeot and the French state on the other hand. I am not one of those who nurture the delusion that the United States is still the archetypal home of classic free enterprise – if it ever was. A good case can be made for the theses that *dirigisme* and state interference in industry run to greater lengths in the USA than in Britain – if you like, that the USA is more 'socialist' than the UK. Notwithstanding, the difference between the American model and the French model is far-reaching and, for our purposes, crucial.

The French state

In France industry is part of the state itself: the major firms in French industry are as much instruments and arms of the French state, serving French national purposes, as if they were units of the French army. Nationalization, subsidies, controls – all the overt instruments of political intervention – though widespread in French industry, are not essential to this truth, which is rooted in the French people and their history. In the France of Philippe Auguste, in the France of Louis XIV, in the France of Charles de Gaulle, the claims and the pre-eminence of the state, albeit under forms to us infinitely more persuasive, civilized, and humane, are no less deep and instinctual than in Russia. Everything that is French is there to serve the purposes of France. Our physical proximity, our admiration, our interwoven histories – I am myself as Francophile as the best – ought not to deceive us as to the almost impassable difference between the nature of the French state and that of our own.

Implications for Chrysler (UK)

The due consequences follow. A Chrysler (UK) which is part of Peugeot would be a part of French industry, and as such it would be part of the French state, in a sense in which it would be laughable to suggest that Chrysler (UK) is part of American industry, or still less, part of the American state.

Nobody can dispute the ruthlessness with which American entrepreneurs and industrialists exploit economic assets at home and, even more, overseas. Nobody at this time of day is unaware that the American government will help them to do so, and will use economic leverage in support of its external policies. The fact remains that Chrysler (UK) in French ownership would belong to a different scene from Chrysler (UK) in American ownership. That scene, if I may use a word of Greek origin which the Chinese are restoring to popularity, is French hegemony in Western Europe, a hegemony economic as well as political. True, it is a hegemony in the making, but a hegemony none the less.

The hegemony of France

The question of Chrysler (UK) merges at this point into the political question to which all roads lead, the political question which subtends every other – that of Britain and the European Economic Community.

Look where you like – to currency, to energy, to steel, to atomic power, to relations with what is called the 'third world' – and you will see the political structure of the EEC being progressively and deliberately used to draw Britain into inextricable attachment – industrially, agriculturally, socially, and economically – to the West European land mass by weakening and then extinguishing its organs of independent self-determination. It is the assertion of continental hegemony over the off-shore island nation; but within that continental hegemony the hegemony of France, which twenty years ago would have been scoffed at as unthinkable, is today a practical and growing reality.

In the web that is being woven quietly, unhurryingly, unceasingly, the purchase of Chrysler (UK) by Peugeot would be one more thread. It is a political and not an economic question, a national and not an industrial question, upon which the British Cabinet have to decide. If they understand, Her Majesty's government will say no.   (Chelsea, 6 September 1978)

In fact, Her Majesty's government said yes; Peugeot assumed control of the company in 1978.

This speech goes a long way to explain why Powell's perception of political and national considerations distance him from those for whom a total lack of intervention is the *only* consideration that matters when defining the economic role of the state. It also has a direct bearing upon Powell's attitude to the economic and trading implications of 1992 – let alone the constitutional aspects.

The speech's key sentence is that which describes the political structure of the EEC as being 'progressively and deliberately used to draw Britain into inextricable attachment ... to the West European land mass by weakening and then extinguishing its organs of independent self-determination.'

There are those who believe that this is what 1992 is also in danger of doing; if so, it is a further example of the extent to which it is misleading to think of it purely in terms of free trade. The so-called global market, which understandably dominates the current thinking of all international companies, may accentuate the economic interdependence of nation states; but it does not impair their right to make or terminate trading agreements, and suffer the consequences. Trade between nations can help determine the economic options that are open to any individual country; it will not, by definition, 'weaken and then extinguish' its independence.

But this, Powell believes, is inherently what the European Community is about; and on this assumption, 1992 can easily be interpreted as no more than part of the general package to draw Britain into an inescapable entanglement with the continental economies.

> What I do find lacking, and alarmingly lacking, is still any understanding of what kind of animal the EEC really is. The British can be terribly naive and ingenuous when dealing with the continental nations – something perhaps due to the live-and-let-live mentality of an island people prone to regard others as basically 'pretty good chaps' like themselves.

So Powell sets out what he regards as the foundations upon which the European Community is built:

> The same France that withdrew from the North Atlantic Treaty Organization, and so remains to this day, despite many predictions to the contrary, understands that the Community rests upon French and German accord and that her leverage is therefore, for practical purposes, unlimited.

He continued:

> The first rule of German statecraft is the maintenance of the Common Market link with France. That may not be ever so; but it is so for the foreseeable future. Germany and France are the Siamese twins of the European Community.
>
> Britain, we ought clearly to understand, all humbug set aside, is expendable. Her function in the Community is to provide the continent with a captive market for dear food, and to place at the disposal of the Community for common use Britain's assets, whether they be the seas around her coasts (the 'Community fish

stocks') or her sources of power (the 'Community energy stocks'). It is not by accident that Britain finds herself the milch cow of Europe: that was the idea of it from the start.

The national interests of France and her in-built bargaining power are buttressed by the appetites common to all the continental members. There is a deep sense and a longer perspective in which the institutions and the policies of the EEC are not merely incompatible with those of Britain but antagonistic. They correspond with the fundamental antagonism between an offshore island and the adjacent continent. In this sense the capture of the United Kingdom by the Common Market represented the reversal of Britain's successful maintenance of her independence since the 16th century: the counter-attack in a new, non-military form had at last succeeded and reduced the historic arbiter of Europe, at least temporarily, to the disarmed status of another European state. The combination of Germany and France, that eventuality dreaded and always frustrated by our forefathers, has produced, albeit under an expected guise, the outcome they foresaw.

(Forfar, 9 November 1979)

Some will feel that this speech is a long way away from the realities of 1992. Powell himself realized that 'the vocabulary I have just been using is so unaccustomed as to make the scene as I describe it appear a flight of fantasy'. The contrast between Powell's and the prevailing view is no where better exemplified than in the speech by Sir Leon Brittan already referred to, where he states that 'British membership is regarded as of such value and of such significance' by the rest of the EEC.

Powell would not necessarily dissent from this view. It is simply that he ascribes different and, from the United Kingdom's point of view, more sinister motives for this interest than would Sir Leon. This also helps to explain why someone who might otherwise be attracted by the idea of a single market is unable to interpret 1992 exclusively in that light.

There is another consideration to be taken into account, even though it does not strictly fall within the bounds of the 1992 debate. There are still those for whom the EEC's greatest purpose and justification is that of defence and Western solidarity. In recent years, Powell has shown increasing determination to challenge conventional strategic thinking, and to question the assumption of a Soviet threat to Western Europe. He has also poured scorn upon NATO's nuclear strategy. But he does not deny that the economic and political forces that are designed to 'integrate' the European economies have strategic implications for Britain's defence. In a speech to the Birmingham branch of the Royal Regiment of Fusiliers Association, he warned:

> The immediate occasion for alarm is the government's announcement that British contractors for supplying armaments to our armed forces must in future share the work with what are called 'European firms', meaning factories situated on the mainland of the European continent.
>
> I ask one question, to which I believe there is no doubt about the answer. What would have been the fate of Britain in 1940 if production of the Hurricane and the Spitfire had been dependent upon the output of factories in France? That a question so glaringly obvious does not get asked in public or in government illuminates the danger created for this nation by the rolling stream of time which bears away the generation of 1940, the generation, that is to say, of those who experienced as adults Britain's great peril and Britain's great deliverance. Talk at Bruges or Luxembourg about not surrendering our national sovereignty is all very well. It means less than nothing when the keys to our national defence are being handed over: an island nation which no longer commands the essential means of defending itself by air and sea is no longer sovereign.

Strategic delusion

That this surrender can take place under our noses with no public protest and even no public awareness is the consequence of a grand strategic delusion into which Britain has allowed itself to be lulled for forty years. The nature of that delusion is Armageddon. We have learnt to believe in a thunderclap war, where our own future as well as that of our allies will be settled by one almighty battle on the Plain of Esdraelon. Whatever may be true for others, that delusion is absolutely fatal for the United Kingdom.

The safety of this island nation reposes upon two pillars. The first is the impregnability of its homeland to invasion by air or sea. The second is its ability and its will to create over time the military forces by which the last conclusive battle will be decided. Without our own industrial base of military armament production neither of those pillars will stand. No doubt, with the oceans kept open, we can look to buy or borrow from the other continents; but to depend on the continent of Europe for our arms is suicide.

For Powell, one of the strategic safeguards of Western Europe is 'the impregnability of the British Isles and the capability of the British nation for military mobilization.'

There is however a condition precedent for that impregnability and that mobilization. It is that Britain retains within itself, un-shared with the European continent, the industrial capability for producing the material equipment indispensable for its defence, and producing it in the order and at the length of notice at which it is likely to be required. What a cruel and foolish irony, that, in the name of our commitment to European peace guaranteed by the balance of power, we should contemplate deliberately divesting ourselves of the one essential contribution that Britain has to make – not to mention the ultimate capability of self-defence, without which liberty and national sovereignty are empty words.

My comrades in the Royal Warwickshire Regiment will understand that if I speak tonight about the material component of British defence, I do so because it is the threat to Europeanize that component which causes most immediate alarm. Of course there is the human component, which, as Napoleon remarked of the moral and the physical, stands to the material factor in the ratio of three to one. The immense expansion which the Royal Warwickshire Regiment underwent in two world wars is part of the proof that Britain has the power, in ways which continental nations do not need to understand, to become in time of need a nation under arms. Of that transformation the line infantry is and will remain the heart and core.

The peacetime army

The proof of Britain's continued will and ability to perform that transformation and perform it as and when called for lies in the peacetime army and in the voluntary peacetime army. The British army, no longer a colonial garrison army, is essentially a cadre army, the peacetime germ of an army at war. Even of this the myth of Armageddon had threatened to deprive us, by representing the voluntary peacetime army as a mere component of regular forces due to be sacrificed to Moloch on the Plain of Esdraelon.

That is false, false to reality, and false to Britain's destiny. Those who serve in peace serve to make possible, and to declare possible, the creation of a future British army comparable with those which defeated the last three bids to erect on military power the mastery of Europe. They are as integral to Britain's liberty as is a British fleet in being and a British armaments industry. Let no passing fashion in international politics deprive us of that defence.

(Birmingham, 18 February 1989)

The debate that centres upon 1992 may appear to have little to do with such grave issues as Britain's defence – although, of course, economic and monetary union would impinge upon this, as upon every other, area. But it is conceivable that Britain's right to maintain the industrial capability necessary to fight a conventional war will be impaired by the economic pressures unleashed by 1992 towards economic convergence. This argument of Powell's is also a further reminder of the extent to which, for him, market forces are not the 'be-all and end-all' of politics.

But 1992 also arouses concerns of a more parochial nature. It has often been said that Powell's arguments ignore the practical realities of the time, and perceive dangers that are more imaginary than real. This characteristic has sometimes alienated him from the more patrician, 'common-sense' Conservatives who, despite sharing his love of England and the nation's institutions, have always distanced themselves from his arguments at the moment when it mattered. It is thus of somewhat ironical amusement that Powell should have chosen one of the country's oldest, and in traditional circles most revered, activities to bring home to an influential minority of the population what 1992 has in store for them.

Who shall decide whether it is to be forbidden by law in Britain to ride to hounds? Why, we, the people of Britain, will decide: it is nobody else's business, and anyhow law is made or amended in this country in Parliament by our representatives whom we elect.

That would be the immediate and indignant answer of the plain citizen – town-dweller or country-dweller. Alas, the plain citizen does not know what has changed while he was taking no notice. He has ceased to be the free citizen of a country governed by those responsible to him in his own free Parliament. John Bull is behind the times. His pants have been removed, though not so far that he cannot get them back if he bestirs himself.

That isn't your boring old carry-on about the Common Market, is it? Yes, my friend, I am afraid it is, and you would be well advised to stop being bored. But what has the Common Market and '1992' and a 'Europe without frontiers' to do with field sports and foxhunting in this country? Brussels and Strasbourg cannot touch my sports, can they? You might imagine not; but I have news for you.

Consider the following assertion made to the European Parliament this year [1988] by one of its committees: 'Completion of the internal market in 1992 implies that significant distortion of competition within the Common Market will cease to exist. This should apply to the tourist sector as well. There is, however, obviously a market for cruel events involving animals. Enormous disparities in animal protection have thus led to distortion of competition which is not compatible with the Common Market. This the Commission must rectify with a draft directive.'

Do not, please, when you read this, dismiss it with a snort, exclaiming: 'What nonsense! Our government will never fall for such twaddle.' You have not realized that the 'internal free market' gives the EEC the power to do more or less anything they like about anything. Here is another bit of reading: 'The obligation to abolish frontiers by 1992 is not what it sounds or is frequently assumed to be. *Any* difference of law, tax, or regulation itself creates a "frontier" and can be deemed to be an impediment to the creation of a single market, even if that "frontier" is not a geographical one. Thus, where national laws differ, they become susceptible to harmonization.'

Do not, pray, seek comfort in the notion that Britain can always vote down or veto any harmonization that we do not like. By a Bill passed under the guillotine by the House of Commons in 1986 we accepted that a European directive to harmonize laws on cruelty to animals or on summer time or any other blessed thing can be carried against us by a majority in the Council of Ministers if it is represented 'to have as its object the establishment or functioning of the internal market'.

Do not make it easy for yourself by objecting: 'But there would never be a majority in the Council of Ministers for harmonizing hunting – or non-hunting.' Have you, my dear sir, never heard of horse-trading, whereby the members of the Council bargain a vote for one thing in return for getting something else? Anyhow, those who already voted to harmonize the standard of bathing beaches will vote to harmonize hunting as soon as look at you.

You may imagine that we could still take such unconscionable decisions to the European Court and ask it to rule that things like this have nothing to do with 'the establishment or functioning of the internal market'. That might be common sense; but the European Court is not in the business of applying common sense to the wording of treaties. It is about extending the scope of the law by using the Court's discretion. As one civil-servant witness, with the inimitable linguistic tact of his kind, informed a Committee of the House of Commons this year, 'the jurisprudence of the Court is *developing* on this particular subject'.

Please do not go just yet. I want you to hear what the European Parliament was told this year about implementation by the EEC of the Berne Convention for the conservation of European wildlife and natural habitats; for are we not all conservation-minded now?

'Whereas, on the one hand, there is no need to prohibit hunting on purely ecological grounds, assuming it does not involve endangered species, on the other hand recreational hunting can be shown to be questionable from an ethical and moral standpoint.'

The conclusion was to invite the Commission 'to lay down legal provisions regulating hunting at Community level'. This conclusion was approved in principle at a plenary session of the Parliament last October by a majority of 176 to 38.

(*The Field*, December 1988)

Powell has been known in the past to argue the intellectual case for blood-sports. It is a practice that he would enthusiastically defend. But even he might be excused for savouring the prospect of certain Tory members of the House of Lords losing their right to hunt due to the implications of 1992.

He once said, 'In thirty years in Parliament I have never seen naked class interest so shamelessly displayed as by those around me who openly declare they prefer to be governed by Brussels sooner than risk the British electorate being able freely to choose politicians and politicians that they fear' (Devizes, July 1978). 'Nemesis' may, according to Powell, be 'notoriously slow'. But there would be poetic justice for the so-called traditional wing of the Conservative party, who voted to remain in the EEC more out of fear of the 'left wing' of the Labour party than for any positive commitment to European union, to have the truth about sovereignty brought home to them through the prohibition of hunting.

There are, however, much bigger issues at stake, which make the come-uppance of certain Tory grandees of no consequence at all. In the speech quoted above, Powell refers to the European Court; and that is another institution destined to play an important part in the process of making 1992 a reality.

CHAPTER FIVE

1992 AND 'THE RULE OF LAW'

If the rule of law is breaking down, it is because our institutions are breaking down.

ENOCH POWELL

The European Court of Justice is charged with the responsibility of upholding the provisions of the treaties upon which the EEC is based. It is not to be confused with the European Court of Human Rights, although both raise, to some extent, similar political considerations. Needless to say, it is these that weigh most heavily with Powell and therefore this chapter deals with his objections to both these institutions.

It is the European Court of Justice that is the most important of the two in the context of the creation of a single market. The United Kingdom has already had direct experience of this reality, notably over VAT. In June 1988 the Court ruled that the zero rating by the United Kingdom of a number of goods and services was not permitted under European Community Law; these included the construction of buildings for industrial and commercial use, water and sewerage services applied to industry, news services supplied to other than final consumers, fuel and power supplied to other than final consumers, and protective boots and helmets purchased by employers.

As the Minister, Peter Lilley, reminded the House of Commons when this ruling was made known, the government 'is obliged to comply' with the detailed terms of the Court's judgment, 'against which there is no right of appeal'. How to *implement* the judgment is left to this country to decide, and the necessary legislative changes were introduced in the 1989 budget. But had the House of Commons refused to accept the changes, then the United Kingdom would have been acting illegally and in contravention of treaties to which it has already submitted by virtue of the European Communities Act, 1972. Also, as Powell points out below, the courts of *this* country would be obliged to enforce Community law should Parliament fail to alter its own statutes in accordance with what the treaties demand.

That is why Lilley, who understands better than most what the EEC is about, was totally justified in saying that 'we have no option but to implement the ruling of the Court, which is a consequence of the treaty obligations that we entered into in 1972 and the subsequent decisions taken in 1977 specifically affecting VAT.' He explained later: 'I do not think that there is much point in criticizing the reasonableness or otherwise of the judgment. It has been made and there is no appeal, and we have to try to implement it as sensitively as possible using such discretion as remains to us' (*Hansard*, 21 June 1988 c. 957–65).

Lilley is right concerning the lack of leeway; but nevertheless interesting questions are involved:

> The general obligation of the citizen to obey the law depends upon the law being duly made. If for instance a Bill had passed only one House of Parliament or had received the Royal Assent in a form different from that in which it had passed both Houses, the citizen would be under no duty to obey it: it would not be law.
>
> The moral force behind that obligation, the unconstrained inner compulsion to obey, derives from the fact that we ourselves have made, and can still unmake and remake, the laws. That statement is a highly metaphorical one. More literally, we identify with ourselves and claim as our own the institutions and the processes by which our law is made, unmade, and remade. We live, so we say, metaphorically again – metaphysically, perhaps – under our own laws: they are flesh of our flesh, bone of our bone.
>
> Of all the members of society this inner imperative is strongest for those who, in a representative capacity, do the institutional work of law-making on behalf of the whole society. Those who make law cannot break law or commend or condone the breaking of law. Otherwise they become a walking self-contradiction.
>
> So far, so good; but suppose that the law is not made by Parliament. Suppose that the Sovereign's enacting words, 'be it

enacted, by and with the advice and consent of the lords spiritual and temporal and commons, in this present parliament assembled, and by authority of the same', have become a lie. Suppose that, by just such an act, the right to make law in this realm has been transferred from our own Parliament to another institution, and that an external, foreign body, and the law-making power is being increasingly exercised by that other legislative authority. What then becomes of my obligation? Can I any longer say to myself: 'These are our laws, we made them, and therefore I must obey them?' Am I not living under a law that has no claims upon my obedience, and ought I not as a free-born Briton to go and break that law and face any consequences? (Belfast, 6 February 1987)

This is a dilemma that Powell, and others who feel like him, increasingly face. He knows the answer to the question; as he reminded his audience on this occasion, the European Communities Act was enacted 'by a still-free Parliament'; and that 'it would be a hopeless prospect to inflict upon ourselves the task of identifying and disobeying only those laws – or identifying and refusing to pay only those taxes – which were imposed as a result of the transfer of legislative and fiscal authority to the European Economic Community.' In any case, 'To live is to live in society; and to live in society is to live under laws.' If Powell and his supporters had refused to live under current UK and EEC laws, 'what laws *were* we going to obey?'

For Powell, therefore, refusing to recognize law enacted by Parliament is not an option, even though it is law that has been made, under powers given to it by Parliament on behalf of the United Kingdom, by an external body. And, although the House of Commons has the theoretical right to ignore the rulings of the European Court of Justice, it can only do so in accordance with law by repealing the Acts that have transferred certain of its powers to this institution. Otherwise it is acting like Wotan in Wagner's *Der Ring des Nibelungen* – in breach of the very rules upon which its authority rests.

But that does not mean that people are obliged to accept this state of affairs for ever, or to welcome the implications. The European Court of Justice will have an increasingly important role to play in making a reality of the single market. This was recognized when the Foreign Affairs Council in October 1988 agreed to proceed with the establishment of a European Court of First Instance in order to help the present Court of Justice handle the anticipated increase in litigation. Thus, the occasions when the House of Commons is prevented from pursuing its most favoured course are bound to increase: the choice will be either to knuckle-under from the beginning, or to test its case in the European Court. But it will be the Court that decides.

We can say in two quite different senses that a society lives under 'the rule of law'. One sense, which an American would recognize but an Englishman would not, is that the law actually occupies the place of the sovereign. As interpreted by its own high priests, the judges, it directs and governs the society and the society's individual members who, beyond those limits, are unconstrained. This meaning of the 'rule of law' requires that 'the law' in question be the unchangeable basis of the society itself. Such a law is the American constitution, which may indeed be amended in accordance with its own provisions but could not be repealed without destroying the state.

Significantly and uncomfortably similar is the Treaty of Rome in relation to that new European state, the EEC: it could be altered by a new treaty agreed by all the parties to it, but if it were abrogated by them there would be no state at all. Even the natural law, or *jus gentium*, which runs through so much continental thinking, must be regarded as eternal and pre-existing, however its interpretation and elaboration may vary. Conceivably, too, that modern monstrosity, 'human rights', since it appeals, like the American Declaration of Independence, to supposed inherent and therefore immutable characteristics of *Homo sapiens*, is of the same brood and likewise immutable.

There is nothing in common between this non-British, or at least non-English, meaning of 'the rule of law' and our own meaning of it. A single question will reveal the contrast. If we were to ask ourselves what act would destroy the British state in the way that repeal of the constitution would destroy the United States or abrogation of the Rome Treaty would destroy the EEC, what would we answer? Not the repeal of any statute, not even the Act of Settlement. It would have to be the abolition of an institution, above all the abolition of that supreme prescriptive institution, the monarchy, of which the sources of authority, Parliament, government, and courts of law, are the organs and manifestations. In short, 'the rule of law' is for us institutional. It is the acceptance of the institutions which validates their handwork – the legislation of Parliament, the acts of the executive both prerogative and statutory, and the decisions and orders of the courts.

Institutional breakdown

We are today anxious about what we call the breakdown of the rule of law. In seeking the causes and thus the remedy we look everywhere except in the right place. If the rule of law is breaking down, it is because our institutions are breaking down. I have used the verb in its intransitive form. I should more accurately say, 'because we have found it possible to break down our institutions'. We have done so partly by abusing them but even more by surrendering them.

The same acceptance of institutions which is the basis of the 'rule of law' in our society implies the rejection of alternative or external authority. The same institutions which exert the magnetic force of authority inside a society imply the denial and repudiation of similar magnetic forces from outside. The affectionate self-identification with a source of authority can by its very nature not be shared between two overlapping or competitive or possibly conflicting authorities.

One source

The nation state is the product of that logic. In England (embracing for this purpose Wales) it was worked out to its final conclusion at the Henrician reformation, the event by which the English nation state was fully realized. All exertion of authority, whether the making or the enforcement of law, the taking of collective decisions of an executive (i.e. not legislable) character, the imposition and collection of taxes, the judgment of causes – in short, all duress brought to bear by the society upon the individual – proceeds from one source, and that source an internal and native one. The England of Henry VIII found it impossible that its laws should be made, that its causes should be judged, or that a revenue should be procured from it by an external authority. In other words, there was no such thing as external authority: the expression was a contradiction in terms.

In the following centuries authority as understood in the English state gained a partial hold upon the mind of the Scots and, even more tenuously, on the northeast of the island of Ireland. The institutions which embodied authority were indeed disputed, re-interpreted, and modified – though as much by way of reaction as of innovation. Authority could be, and was, challenged from within the state by the principle of 'private judgment', which achieved toleration in the spiritual sphere of society, but by no means in the temporal. Still, the notion of an external authority remained inapprehensible to British minds: the idea was literally foreign – one could not both entertain it and continue to belong.

The United Nations

Then, quite suddenly, after the Second World War, four hundred years on from the Henrician declaration of independence, author-ity began to collapse. At first what was happening was scarcely noticed; but after a generation the cumulative revolution that has occurred is undisputable and imposing. What for four centuries was literally unthinkable has already become commonplace.

In 1946 Parliament enacted that any change in the law neces-sary to comply with a mandatory resolution of the United Nations was to be made not by Act of Parliament but by an Order in Council. Apart from having to be 'laid' before Parliament, such orders, which were of the most comprehensive scope – 'such pro-vision as appears necessary or expedient, including provision for the apprehension, trial, and punishment of persons offending' – were subject to no parliamentary process or control whatever. They would have been intolerable to Charles I's Long Parliament as exercise of the royal prerogative. But they were authorized in 1946 with barely a murmur, thus giving virtually direct and unlim-ited power in this kingdom to an external Leviathan. Twenty years later the Act was used – when Britain called in the United Nations to help it coerce Rhodesia.

European Convention of Human Rights

In 1951 Parliament provided, by ratifying the European Conven-tion on Human Rights without debate, that both the Crown itself and any of its subjects within the realm, corporate or personal, could be arraigned and judged before an external court, which could give orders accordingly. Again twenty years elapsed before recourse began to be had to this external, superior jurisdiction; but when it was, the consequences of our own handiwork stood revealed. What the England of Henry VIII and Elizabeth I had repudiated, the possibility that any external tribunal could

> 'task to interrogatories
> The free breath of a sacr'd king',

had been conceded, almost unawares.

Today individual citizens, local authorities, companies, trade unions, as soon as they are dissatisfied with the laws or judgments or decisions of the institutions of their own country, are to be seen crossing the sea in droves to appeal to a foreign institution, a commission and a court which sit in judgment over the supreme institutions of this realm and hand down orders which we have bound ourselves to obey. Why, even the servants of the Crown itself, if they get a favourable decision in that tribunal, deck themselves in it with pride and satisfaction, as witness the Secretary of State for Northern Ireland [Humphrey Atkins] proclaiming to all and sundry that the European Court of Human Rights has upheld Her Majesty against the claims of the murderers confined in her prison at the Maze.

Treason

There is a name for appealing over the head of the Crown to an authority outside the realm, and that name is treason. The word may be disused, but the thing is not; and the penalties of *praemunire*, which those guilty of it formerly incurred, were not disproportionate to its seriousness. Consciously or not, the British people have withdrawn acceptance from their institutions in favour of institutions which are not theirs. It was consequently a thing not totally unprepared when in 1972 the Crown in Parliament made a comprehensive surrender to an external power of all the aspects of sovereignty, domestic and foreign, from the right to conclude treaties to the right to tax, from the right to make laws to the right to judge causes. This price of admission to the European

Economic Community was paid, not indeed without debate or opposition, but by a Parliament and a public prepared to treat with ridicule as obsolete the question of authority itself, of the external sovereignty of the state. 'Authority,' it is said, 'deserts a dying king.' It certainly deserts an abdicating king. The last generation has witnessed a deliberate and comprehensive abdication of authority by the institutions which were its vehicle.

Not merely do external institutions now tax, legislate, and judge causes in Britain, but the courts of this country will enforce the law of the European Community, if Parliament fails to pass or to enact the necessary legislation. It may be wondered what basis for the rule of law can be afforded by institutions which have themselves publicly abdicated. The citizens, once again, have taken the lesson to heart. No discontent, no dissatisfaction, no deficiency so trivial or so important, but that politicians and public representatives, mayors in their chains and lawyers in their gowns, join the throng of suitors at the imperial court to lay their grievances and claim redress from the new Caesar. Small wonder if the law is despised when the native institutions which should make and uphold it have despised themselves.

(Lancaster, 8 November 1980)

Lord Young took satisfaction in pointing out, during a lecture he delivered to the Royal Society of Arts in February 1989, that Britain enjoys a very good record so far as the European Court is concerned. 'Over the past ten years,' he said, 'only Denmark has had fewer complaints to the Commission and references to the European Court of Justice than Britain.' What is more, 'when we have had adverse judgments from the European Court of Justice, we have acted on them ... our record in implementing Community decisions is better than most other member states.' From this, it must be concluded that the political world in which Lord Young lives knows nothing of the disgust with which such statements are received by those of his fellow citizens who revere this country's institutions as Powell does.

An almost weekly occurrence is now the handing down of judgments from a European Court which either overturns the judgments of our own courts or rules against our own legislation and requires Parliament to make or amend the law to accord with those decisions.

It is hard for anyone who retains any vestige of national pride or attachment to comprehend the mentality of those who, cheerfully and without any apparent sense of shame, if dissatisfied with the law or the courts of their own country, push off to the continent to seek to have Parliament or the Crown overruled. So far, however, from such persons being shunned or despised, their conduct appears to be received with at least equanimity, if not approbation; and in case it be argued that this is a disagreeable and unexpected consequence of Britain having adhered to the Convention of Human Rights in 1951 under the impression that it was a mere exercise in humbug, the renewal of the right of individual application to the European Court was approved by Parliament within this year – without debate, not to mention division. Yet a state whose citizens can plead their case against it in a foreign court has no claim to be a nation.   (Essex, 30 October 1981)

Powell has devoted much more attention to the European Court of Human Rights than to the European Court of Justice. The reasons for this fall outside the ambit of this book, embracing, as they do, the whole basis of universal rights and the extent to which individuals should be allowed to appeal beyond the limits of their own national societies.

The two courts are distinct, although each member state of the EEC recognizes the jurisdiction of the European Court of Human Rights in human-rights cases. The European Court of Justice, however, is expected to deal with more mundane matters – such as the resolution of all kinds of disputes within the Community by reference to the Treaties.

It is debatable to what extent the Court merely upholds the rules of 'the club' or, on occasions, actually extends them. This is because the Court is also expected to take account of the lawmakers' *intentions* in a way that is foreign to those brought up under the English tradition. Nevertheless, the Court's remit is specific – the enforcement and, where necessary, the interpretation of the Treaties.

In the past, agricultural disputes have dominated the Court's deliberations – bearing witness to the fact that the Common Agricultural Policy was, until recently, the political area in which the Community had reached its fullest development. The creation of the single market by the end of 1992 will widen the Court's horizons considerably.

But the Court's existence is, unlike that of the European Court of Human Rights, an inevitable consequence of the European Community's formation and rationale. It is no more than a symptom of the malaise that haunts so many of Powell's speeches upon this, and other, subjects. In particular, and as we have seen, it is unimaginable to Powell that any United Kingdom citizen should wish to appeal to authority outside his own country. Recently, however, Powell has detected grounds for optimism.

> It was the authority of Parliament which James II had unsuccessfully challenged, and – in England at least – it was the authority of Parliament in which the nation at large was content, and remained content until after the Second World War, to repose its trust. As the barons had acted for 'the community of the realm' in the 13th century when Magna Carta, the Great Charter, was extorted, it was Parliament, not yet elected by more than a small fraction of the adult population, which spoke and acted, and was assumed to speak and act, for the nation at large in 1688–9. The rights vindicated in 1689 were the rights of a parliamentary nation, the rights implicit in being governed, taxed, and judged by the advice and consent of Parliament – no less and no more.
>
> Three hundred years later, almost precisely, the nation in whose Parliament not only England but Scotland and Northern Ireland are now content to be represented, is invited to say whether it will relinquish its right to be governed, taxed, and judged under Parliament in order to be governed by bodies representative of other nations and under laws interpreted by courts which overrule Parliament.
>
> In recent years the nation's leaders have taught it to imagine that the question could be dodged. The Crown's Ministers have made treaties with other countries in which they promised that Parliament should be silenced or overborne. Sometimes the thing was done without demur, as when, with no debate in Parliament, Britain acknowledged the European Court of Human Rights as superior to Parliament and to the courts of this realm. Sometimes there was protracted debate, as when Britain acceded to the Treaty of Rome in 1973 and to the Single European Act in 1986. [In fact both pieces of legislation were subject to the guillotine and the Bill to enact the Single European Act received only some forty hours of discussion in committee on the floor of the House of Commons.]

Whose authority?

Now in 1989 that phase is coming to an end. The Queen's Chief Minister has told Europe that power must remain with national parliaments. [Margaret Thatcher at Bruges said that there was no requirement for 'power to be centralized in Brussels or decisions to be taken by an appointed bureaucracy'; she also wished to preserve 'the different traditions, Parliamentary powers, and sense of national pride in one's own country'.]

The Queen's Home Secretary has announced that Parliament will legislate irrespective of the European Court. The question of 1689 had not gone away; for it never can go away from a free people. It is indeed the most fundamental of all political questions. It is the question: upon whose authority will we consent to be governed?

The question is rightly posed in the plural: 'we'. The answer to it, as to so many fundamental human questions, is a circularity: 'we' are satisfactorily definable only as those who consent to be governed by this particular authority. 'We' is not an aggregation of individuals, each of whom is endowed simply by being a human with enforceable claims – commonly called rights – as against other human beings.

Declaration of Right

That may have been the sort of theory to which some of the men who organized the accession of William and Mary would have appealed. It is a theory which their words and actions repudiated. When, in the words of the Declaration of Rights, they 'claimed, demanded, and insisted upon their undoubted rights and liberties', the rights and liberties were those that would be 'strengthened and preserved' by the institution which James II had endeavoured to undermine and which 'His Highness the Prince of Orange' had proved to be the means of reinstating in what were regarded as its immemorial powers and privileges.

What those men could not have conceived was that their successors three hundred years later, having attributed 'rights and liberties' to individuals as human beings, would then endeavour to secure those 'rights and liberties' by endowing authorities outside the kingdom with the function of overruling Parliament and exercising inside Britain the powers of taxation, legislation, and government. In giving 'the force of law' to the Declaration of Rights – the terms and conditions on which the Crown was offered and accepted on 13 February, 1689 – the Lords and Commons in October 1689 'declared and enacted that all and singular the rights and liberties asserted and claimed' in the Declaration 'are *the true and ancient and indubitable rights and liberties of the people of this kingdom'*. So inseparable did they consider those rights to be from the collectivity of the nation as represented in Parliament.

In 1989 we survey the logical results of having in our own day attempted to create a separation. New authorities have been called into existence to supersede the Parliament of this kingdom and to define and enforce new rights and liberties. What remains to be seen is whether 'the people of this kingdom' accept those authorities. If they do, they have lost their 'true ancient and indubitable rights and liberties' and acquired none in exchange. Not even the French in 1789 did that.   (*Daily Telegraph*, 4 January 1989)

CHAPTER SIX

THE AMERICAN CONNECTION

No government can hold office in contemporary Britain unless it conforms with the assumptions of United States strategic policy.

ENOCH POWELL

Political issues cannot easily be compartmentalized; and if it is reasonable to assert that more is implied by 1992 than the mere creation of a single market, it follows that wider questions may also be germane to the debate. Powell would argue that the policies and strategic objectives of the United States of America fall into this category.

This book is making no attempt to illustrate the entirety of Powell's political beliefs; if it were, his hostility towards the United States – which has become much more pronounced in recent years – would need to be analysed and explained in depth.

But what needs to be understood in the context of 1992 is that at no time has Powell's attitude towards the EEC been rooted in a preference for closer links with America. It is inconceivable that he would ever have used the words chosen by Margaret Thatcher to conclude her speech at Bruges: 'Let us have a Europe which plays its full part in the wider world, which looks outward not inward, and which preserves that Atlantic Community – that Europe on both sides of the Atlantic – which is our noblest inheritance and our greatest strength.'

'*Europe on both sides of the Atlantic*' is not a phrase that could be uttered by Powell. His devotion to Europe as something unique runs counter to all that is symbolized by the statement. As long ago as 1969, when Powell began seriously to express his misgivings over Britain's membership of the EEC, he asserted 'I am what is called 'a European'.' Two years later, he laid his credentials for saying so firmly on the table:

> It is as a European among Europeans that I claim to speak to you. Both in the years when I was my party's official spokesman on defence, and also before and since, I have always argued that Britain's commitment to the alliance with her continental neighbours is second only in importance to the commitment to the air and maritime defence of her own islands. In fact, my stress upon the continental commitment of Britain's main forces got me into frequent troubles with the 'East of Suez' brigade.
>
> In particular I am passionately francophile, and have for many years believed and publicly stated that a breach in understanding between France and Britain could have as serious consequences in the future as it has actually twice produced during the present century. The profound differences of social, cultural, and political idiom between our nations conceal the identity of our devotion to individual liberty: I would dare to say that there is no third nation in the world which shares with us the same meaning and the same instinctive valuation of personal freedom.

This is vintage Powell. It hardly accords with the image fostered by enthusiasts of Britain's membership, who like to portray their opponents as never having travelled beyond Dover; and of course the words used by Powell betray no secret admiration of the New World. He has none. Indeed, Powell's love of France is matched by his lack of sympathy for what the United States stands for. In this sense he is far removed from the tradition inherited from Churchill, although he would have agreed with Churchill when he declared that England is 'with Europe, but not of it'.

To demonstrate Powell's commitment to Europe further:

> From boyhood I have been devoted to the understanding of that Greek and Roman inheritance, which, in varying measure, is common to all that is Europe, and not only the 'Europe' of the six or eight or ten, but Europe from the Atlantic to the Urals – and beyond.
>
> I also claim that reverent enthusiasm for the history of my own country which commands an equal reverence for the past that

has formed everything else which is European. The truest European, in my opinion, is the man who is most humbly conscious of the vast demands which comprehension of even a little part of this Europe imposes upon those who seek it; for the deeper we penetrate, the more the marvellous differentiation of human society within this single continent evokes our wonder. The very use of the word 'Europe' in expressions like 'European unity', 'going into Europe', 'Europe's role in the world' is a solecism which grates upon the ear of all true Europeans.

(Lyons, 12 February 1971)

Nearly twenty years later Margaret Thatcher was to make a similar point at Bruges. In what has become one of the required texts of the whole 1992 debate, she said 'Europe is not the creation of the Treaty of Rome'. She also said: 'the European Community is *one* manifestation of that European identity. But it is not the only one. We must never forget that, East of the Iron Curtain, peoples who once enjoyed a full share of European culture, freedom, and identity have been cut off from their roots. We shall always look on Warsaw, Prague, and Budapest as great European cities.' Re-reading Powell's speeches of twenty years ago, it is as if he had designed Margaret Thatcher's clothes twenty years before she put them on.

Certainly Powell attaches significance to her words today. He believes that they reflect a growing acceptance in the Foreign Office and elsewhere of a view of the world – and of defence strategy – that he has often espoused in the past. But, as we have seen, there is still one area of considerable disagreement. Margaret Thatcher has regarded the NATO alliance – and Britain's alliance with the United States, in particular – as of primary importance. Powell believes it has been destructive of Britain's self-confidence and interests.

His rejection of the hypothesis upon which the nuclear strategy rests is an issue in itself. But few would deny that *perestroika* has given extra weight to his argument that the Soviet Union poses no real threat to Western Europe's security.

What is at issue in the context of 1992, however, is how all this affects Britain's wider relations with the United States. Inevitably, the special responsibility for the defence of Western Europe shouldered by the United States since the war has spilled over into other areas; take defence away, and the United States would popularly be seen more in terms of an economic rival than an honorary member of Europe.

Powell's distrust of United States strategic policy was apparent before 1956, but it was Suez that confirmed his opposition to 'the special relationship', of which he had always been sceptical. His distrust became much more pronounced and pervasive once Powell became immersed in the battle to defend Northern Ireland's place within the United Kingdom.

His analysis of the problem convinced him that, in this war at least, the United States was not so much indifferent as to the outcome but was actually fighting on the side of Ulster's enemies. This view is not universally shared by those who otherwise support Powell's basic approach. But Powell's own strategy has been built upon the conviction that the United States is happy to see the unification of Ireland outside the United Kingdom if this is the price to be paid for ending Eire's neutrality.

This gave him an added reason for expressing the conviction that Britain was both needlessly and dangerously associated with all that the United States stood for.

> The thesis that I lay before you this morning is one at which I arrived reluctantly and painfully yet with cumulative conviction as I lived, observing and reflecting, through the political vicissitudes of the 1970s and 1980s. I will formulate the thesis at the outset. It runs as follows: 'No government can hold office in contemporary Britain unless it conforms with the assumptions of United States strategic policy.' Since all necessity resides in the mind, the thesis may be re-stated slightly differently thus: 'No government in contemporary Britain *believes* it can hold office unless it conforms with the assumptions of United States strategic policy.'

Powell's justification for this assertion was founded upon a whole range of United States policies – including her trading relations with the rest of the world, her role in the International Monetary Fund and the World Bank, and in Ulster. But a crucial element in this speech's argument involved NATO; and NATO, Powell believes, is integral to what the EEC is all about. Thus the link between NATO, the EEC, and 1992 now becomes, under Powell's reasoning, apparent.

> At the beginning of next year [1986] Spain and Portugal will become members of the European Economic Community. There is no benefit in this for the existing EEC members. On the contrary, they will in varying degrees be laid under contribution to subsi-

dize the Spanish and Portuguese economies, and the uneasy financial relationships among themselves, which they have just with great difficulty managed to settle, will be thrown into disarray.'

Powell's prediction was to prove well founded. The accession of Spain and Portugal in January 1986 threw the arrangement agreed at Fontainebleau in June 1984 into confusion. It had been at this summit that 'permanent' arrangements were agreed to reduce the United Kingdom's EEC budget contribution; an increased 'own resources' ceiling for the whole Community was also introduced. The consequent increase in the VAT ceiling, however, still turned out to be inadequate after enlargement; emergency measures became necessary to balance the 1987 budget, and further acrimonious discussions ensued, culminating in the Copenhagen Summit in December 1987. As Neil Kinnock argued at the time, Fontainebleau had proved 'neither effective nor disciplined and certainly not lasting'. (*Hansard*, 8 December 1987 c. 168)

Powell went on:

> So why did this unnatural event occur? Spain became a member of the American alliance known as NATO in May 1982 against the strong disinclination of a large part of its people. A referendum next spring could take Spain out of NATO again. [In fact, a comfortable majority voted to remain within the alliance.] At the critical stage of the negotiation with the EEC the Spanish premier deployed the slogan: 'No membership of the EEC, no membership of NATO.'
>
> The present premier, Signor Gonzales, whose party campaigned against membership of NATO, was warned of the continuing force of that slogan at the beginning of this month when Chancellor Kohl, we are told, 'emphasized the link between EEC membership and NATO'. The link is simple: the benefits extended by the other members are the price to be paid for an Iberian peninsula in the American alliance. And why do the European countries pay up? Because the requirements of American geo-politics are regarded by them as mandatory.

A relentless strategic imperative

The same theorem explains the story of the EEC and Greece,

whose Prime Minister also changed his mind about the Common Market after coming into office.

Talking of change of mind makes one feel, all of a sudden, quite at home. It reminds one of three Labour party leaders in a line, Wilson, Callaghan, Kinnock. In 1974 Wilson and Callaghan moved into No. 10 and the Foreign Office firmly committed against British membership of the Common Market. Within a month they were standing on their heads, a new light had dawned, another imperative had become dominant.

The innocent may imagine that they worked out the economic sums again and got a different answer – but Kinnock? What source of economic enlightenment caused him, on becoming Labour's leader after a lost election, to drop overboard as his first act the official, long-standing, and detailed Labour party commitment to quit the Community? He bowed to the same relentless strategic imperative which none before him has been able to resist.

The Foreign Office

A fascinating glimpse behind the scenes was vouchsafed a year ago by Sir Anthony Parsons, an eminent ex-Foreign Office official and civil servant. In a Sunday newspaper he wrote applauding a colleague's stated opinion that 'a severe strain would be imposed on the code of loyal service to political masters if a future government were to adopt an extremely radical policy' – what sort of 'radical policy'? – 'such as withdrawal from the European Community or from NATO'.

The juxtaposition is significant. In American eyes the European Community, tiresome though some of its economic consequences may be, is the indispensable political counterpart of NATO. Hence the increasing stress being laid upon the non-economic and external political significance of the Community. Hence the revealing assertion that Sir Anthony Parsons went on to make, that 'if the broad bipartisanship of the past forty years broke down in such a way, many officials in the higher reaches of the Foreign Office would find it impossible conscientiously to implement the new policies and the government would be obliged to recruit political loyalists in order to carry out its will.

(Eastbourne, 18 October 1985)

Powell had emphasized the defence implications before:

> Let nobody bluff you, as we used to bluff ourselves in the early
> 1970s, with the idea that the EEC has nothing to do with defence.
> We never quite understood – did we? – why its advocates in those
> days insisted on claiming that membership of the EEC was integral
> to Britain's security. Well, here is the answer, as one so often finds
> the solution to conundrums by jobbing backwards from subse-
> quent events, and the answer is this: the EEC, which from the
> United States point of view was the reverse of a good thing
> economically, was for them a politico-strategic necessity. Did you
> not notice that Spain's bargaining counter, when negotiating to
> join the Community, was 'If we don't join the EEC, we won't stay
> linked to NATO, and the Americans can take their forces and their
> bases out of Spain'?
>
> When the Foreign Office negotiated Britain into the Commu-
> nity and Edward Heath imposed the result upon Parliament, they
> were not, as they purported at the time, 'speaking for Britain' nor
> acting off their own bat. They were carrying into execution one
> part of that American 'grand design', to which official Britain has
> been committed these forty years.

He concluded:

> When you and I battle to preserve and regain Britain's unique par-
> liamentary independence and national sovereignty by 'getting
> Britain out', the opponents visibly ranged against us consist only
> of a thin screen of satellite forces. Behind and above them loom
> the beetling battlements of world-infatuated Super Power
> America, manned by the hosts of officialdom who will shoot their
> employers in the back if they even dream of giving in to us or
> running away. Our warfare is against 'principalities and powers',
> the forces and influences which hindsight reveals as the true archi-
> tects and masterminds of Britain's great renunciation in 1972.
> (London, 11 May 1985)

Powell's critics will dismiss this as the old conspiracy theory of politics. But
if it is true that the EEC is so tied up with United States strategic objectives,
then it must also be true that 1992 is similarly entwined. As we have seen,

there are those who believe that *political* objectives are behind the creation of a single market. Anything, therefore, that lessens the attractiveness of the NATO alliance might do the same for 1992 and the principles behind the EEC.

This may seem a somewhat tortuous argument, particularly given the ability of both France and the Republic of Ireland to remain outside NATO and still remain within the European Community. But it is in any case very difficult – if not impossible – for anyone outside government to make an informed appraisal of Powell's case so far as United States intentions are concerned. The validity or otherwise of his assertions may one day become apparent. What is certain is that no recent member of any administration would publicly admit the smallest credence to Powell's thesis.

On the other hand, it is equally the case that many advocates of Britain's membership of the EEC would agree that Britain has, since the Second World War, tied herself too closely to the interests of America. They might not go the whole way with Powell, particularly with regard to Ulster. But they would accept that Britain needs to distance herself from United States foreign policy, which in some respects runs counter to British objectives.

The problem, however, is that they do not agree with Powell that Britain can do this by herself. They perceive a necessary and inescapable role for the whole of the EEC if the balance is to be redressed. Indeed, part of the rationale behind political union is to enable the EEC to become a 'world player' on the international stage in its own right. That is what lies behind the idea that Europe should speak 'with one voice', and develop its own independent and individual position upon world affairs. This is something again to which Powell is fundamentally opposed.

The Rome Treaty actually makes no mention of foreign policy; but the desire to co-ordinate policy in this area has been evident for at least twenty years, and the Single European Act (Article 30) commits the member states to 'endeavour jointly to formulate and implement a European foreign policy'.

Not a great deal of success has been achieved in this area up to now. On occasions, the Community has agreed to the common imposition of economic sanctions – for example against Israel, Iran, the Soviet Union, and South Africa (although in this last case only after much heart-searching by Britain and modification of the original proposals). It is questionable whether such initiatives have had any detrimental effect upon the countries against whom these sanctions were directed.

More ambitiously, the Community has on occasions attempted to 'launch initiatives' and propose solutions to some of the more intransigent problems of international affairs. One of these earliest attempts, in 1980, was known as the Venice Declaration on the Middle East. Powell was merciless in his criticism of what this Declaration said and purported to achieve. He believed it committed the EEC 'to two sets of principles which are meaningless in abstraction from physical power and which are inherently contradictory, so that the one could not be realized except at the expense of the other'; and he continued, 'The EEC announces that it will promote a peace settlement in the Middle East on untenable principles and will uphold it with an unthinkable commitment.'

He was even more contemptuous of the fact that the EEC had attempted an initiative in the first place. His remarks concluded in this way:

> How on earth did we come to be mixed up in such lunacy? The answer to that question can be summed up in two words: delusion and ambition.
>
> The delusion is well conveyed in the introductory paragraph of the Declaration: 'the traditional ties and common interests which link Europe to the Middle East oblige' — note the word 'oblige' — 'them (i.e. the EEC) to play a special role, and now require them' — note the word 'require' — 'to work in a more concrete way towards peace.'
>
> Of course, circumstances in *any* part of the world are in some way or to some extent of interest in *all* other parts of the world; and where the volume of material trade is considerable, that will be necessarily so. But interest in this sense is quite distinct from interest in the sense which obliges, requires, justifies, and makes practicable political and physical intervention.
>
> Interest in this latter sense only exists where political and physical integrity and security are involved, and so directly involved that the threat or use of force is rational and practical. That is where the Belgian guarantee [the guarantee of Belgian neutrality that bound Britain and her allies in 1914], which touched the direct territorial and military safety of the guarantors, differed so essentially from the guarantee that features in the Declaration of the EEC.

Naked force

As clearly as anywhere in the world, the borders and positions in the Middle East represent the local balance of naked force and will be altered only by an alteration in that balance. Israel owes its very existence to successful force; and the present boundaries of its effective territory, though far short of 'secure' or 'recognized', are also the standing monument to force successfully exerted.

I once described Israel as the Prussia of the Middle East; and the analogy of a small and poor state improbably surviving by military success and external subsidies is not inapt. The idea of Britain and the Grand Duchy of Luxembourg, even in combination, setting out to alter the configuration of forces in the Levant is ludicrous; there is no interest, either of this kingdom or that duchy, which would authorize or render credible the exertion of that force that would be necessary. If 'peace' and 'settlement', whatever those terms mean, arrive in 'the Middle East', however that area is defined, it will be because the local balance of forces, present or future, attains a degree of *de facto* permanence.

Statehood

My other explanatory word was 'ambition'. The Venice Declaration is an exhibition of the inordinate and unsatisfied craving of the European Economic Community to behave as a state and eventually to approximate more and more to statehood, superseding the pre-existing national sovereignties. Somewhat checked in its approach to this goal by the route of economic unification, the Community is switching to the easier approach route of unified external politics.

When I call that route easier, I mean only that it is easier at first, as long as acts of foreign policy consist in wordy declarations like that on the Middle East, which provide the heads of government with a cheap and welcome opportunity to intersperse their quarrels about real economic interests with verbose and meaningless acts of political unanimity.

Like all humbug and deception of oneself and of others, this device has its cost, and the cost is a steep one. The renunciation of a national foreign policy in favour of the EEC is not a less but a greater renunciation than that of agricultural or monetary or economic policy. There is no reason at all why the true interests of the UK in the Middle East should coincide with those of France, Germany, or the Grand Duchy of Luxembourg — rather the presumption is to the contrary — and an EEC foreign policy, in the Middle East or elsewhere, will not be a British foreign policy.

(Surrey, 5 August 1980)

So Powell makes the case for an independent and distinct foreign policy — distinct from that of the United States and divorced from anything that the EEC may be hoping to achieve.

But this is not to be taken as a denial that Britain's essential interests are in Europe. Powell believes that the 'twin pillars' upon which United States ascendancy was built — the the presumed aggressive intentions of Soviet Russia towards Western Europe and the consequent need for NATO — have now been swept away. Thus,

in this new Europe which succeeds the collapse of the American Empire a new balance of power will replace the vanished balance of nuclear terror and will create, not without historical precedent, a structure inside which the future pattern of central Europe can emerge without disastrous consequences for the rest of Europe and the world. (*Guardian*, 7 December 1988)

This last quotation brings us up to date with Powell's current position. The speeches quoted above demonstrate how Powell defines 'Europe' and 'Europeans'; how he regards United States influence as destructive of British interests; but how nevertheless he deplores any attempt of the EEC to formulate its own foreign policy. He has also argued that, despite protestations to the contrary, the EEC is to do with defence and is tied up with the interests of NATO.

Perestroika, however, has challenged all the assumptions upon which NATO is based. It follows, therefore, that major forces are at work that will demand fresh thinking across the whole spectrum of international affairs. The EEC cannot escape this inevitable process of reappraisal. 'The future pattern of central Europe' that Powell foresees has major implications for the assumptions that were implicit in the EEC's formation and are still implied by its continued existence.

We British are naughty about history. Smugly satisfied with 'our rough island story', we doubt if other people ought to think about history at all or indeed whether they have any history worth thinking about.

Well, they have, and they do; and as Europe imagines it catches sight of spring around the corner, they will be remembering a piece of history which I am afraid tends to move Englishmen to foolish mirth. They will be remembering the Holy Roman Empire. When the laughter has subsided, I will try to explain why.

People's memories in Czechoslovakia, in Austria, and in Hungary run back beyond the Wilsonian re-drawing of the map of Europe on a preconceived pattern of nationalities identified by plebiscite. They run back beyond the Austria-Hungary which precipitated and participated in the German catastrophe of 1914–18. They leap across the Hohenzollern Empire which Prussia erected by dint of military victory upon the foundations of the North and South German Confederacies.

An older empire

Behind all this, they recollect an older empire, whose title and prestige the Prussians acquired – the empire dismembered by the campaigns of Napoleon and revolutionary France, the empire which the last *Augustus*, Francis II, abdicated in 1806.

His predecessor, Joseph, had been elected King of the Romans as imperial heir-apparent in Frankfurt in 1764 with all the traditional pomp. I remember how deeply struck I was on first reading – at Frankfurt, as it happened – Goethe's account of that election in his autobiography, *Poetry and Reality*. There was a universal quality in the empire's claim which overrode other loyalties without suppressing them. Its ghost haunts Europe still. In taking leave of this theme, James Bryce, the historian of the *Holy Roman Empire*, wrote of feeling 'that words fail to convey the ideas it suggests and that, however much may have been said, much must remain unsaid because incapable of expression.' No wonder if it be still lodged in the memory of the peoples of Central Europe.

Central Europe

Of course, like any ghost, the empire will not put on flesh and blood again. A past remembered is not a past resurrected. That does not mean that ghosts and memories do not affect men's minds as they address themselves to the great questions opened up by the events of 1987 for the first time in forty years. Since the late 1940s, it has not been necessary to think about the future of Central Europe. The Iron Curtain, and the balance of mutual terror which was believed to sustain it, excused everyone, East or West, from the inconvenience of needing to think. The division of Germany and the anomaly of Berlin could be treated light-heartedly as examples of 'the provisional which lasts forever'. The future of the Danubian states needed to be projected only in such terms as Foster Dulles would have understood.

Now suddenly these questions have become alive, real, and acute. People are thinking about Central Europe again. They are thinking about it again in Whitehall. They are thinking about it again in Central Europe itself. They are thinking about it in Moscow. Let no one imagine the Russians were unaware this would be the consequence when they decided — it *was* the Russians who decided — to give the old permafrost a bit of a thaw.

Says Serge to Ivan one day in the Kremlin: 'Ivan, I've been reflecting on all this business in Afghanistan. Tell me, do you really think there will ever again be a Czechoslovakia 1968?'

'I was wondering just the same thing myself, Serge. Frankly, my answer is, "No, there will not. I cannot imagine our proceeding in that manner again." And now, you tell me: do you really think that there will ever again be a Hungary 1956?'

'Candidly, Ivan, I don't. So, comrade, what happens in Central Europe and what in particular happens about West Germany, East Germany, and Berlin? Do you know, a funny thing happened to me when I was musing about this and looking at a map. I noticed a spot on it marked "British Isles", and I said to myself: "Laddie, the people who live there must be seeing exactly what I'm seeing, only upside down".'

A united Germany

Like opening gambits in chess, the early stages are delusively simple. A Germany no longer divided would not, geographically or otherwise, be the Third Reich which invaded Poland in 1939. For one thing, it would not be Bismarck's Prussian Empire on which fell the cloak of the Holy Roman Empire ownerless since Austria's defeat at Königgrätz in 1866; nor would it be the Germany of Hitler, which absorbed Austria in 1938. To venture another step into the perils of the obvious, Bohemia, Hungary, and the Balkans are not going to re-stage the pantomime of the pseudo-democratized Austrian Empire nor rehearse the unhappy stories of the years before Sarajevo.

Europe without the Americans

On the other hand, the spectacle of a group of isolated nations looks both improbable and unstable. It may be wise at this stage to say nothing less vague than that a *tertium quid* of some sort would appear to be indicated. That *tertium quid* would not be, and could not be, represented as being a reincarnation of the Holy Roman Empire. Yet the fact and the memory of that empire, the disembodied ghost of it, could be a good fairy at the cradle.

So much may be hazarded without absurdity about the Europe which all the governments concerned are now privately daring to imagine: a Europe without the Americans. To go further would be to tumble into the silly game of playing with nations like chessmen on a board. Events have a way of shaping themselves into forms the historian recognizes only in retrospect. After forty years of imprisonment in a moral and military stereotype, what the continental nations will want to do is to reflect upon their future place in the new scene beginning to unfold. The British, though under less duress perhaps, have been as closely imprisoned as any. They need not only to summon to their assistance the recollection of their own history, but to submit themselves to the discipline of trying to get inside the mind and memory of nations which they have too long kept outside the purlieus of their attention.

(*Independent*, 13 May 1988)

The creation of a single market in Europe may seem light years away from the train of thought opened up by Powell in the extract just quoted above. The main point of Powell's argument, however, is that things are happening in Europe that could demolish the very foundations upon which the EEC is built; and in this event, to use common parlance, 'all bets would be off'.

But Powell is only developing here an argument which, on a less exalted scale, he discussed at the time of Britain's accession. *Perestroika*, still less *glasnost*, had not even been mentioned when Powell requested an audience in Germany to consider the implications for the European Community of a Germany no longer divided; what then might have seemed almost a perverse distraction has now become a practical question.

> So far as conflict between the countries of the Community is concerned, the sole prospect which causes apprehension is that of a recreation of German power in Central Europe, however remote reunification may seem.
>
> If this occurred at all, it surely could not happen by the inclusion of East Germany — and perhaps other central European countries — in a politically united Western Europe: the resultant giant state would be too unwieldy and disparate to survive, or too menacing to be tolerated, particularly by its neighbours on the East. The unexpressed intention must therefore be that the Community's existence would permanently exclude or prevent reunification, and would be more likely to succeed if it included Britain.
>
> I dissent again. In the first place, I do not believe West Germany in the Community can either forget or renounce reunification. Without wishing to ignore any of the complexities and qualifications, it is simply not credible that a new unification of Western Europe will obliterate an older unity which has such powerful historical and geographical forces beneath it. It would not be made any more credible by the mere fact that Britain belonged to that new West European unity.
>
> This does not mean that Britain belonging or not would be of no importance. In framing the new balance of power which would be necessary if this development was to take place without catastrophe, it seems to me that a Britain not indissolubly embodied politically in the adjacent continent would be useful, if not indispensable.   (Frankfurt am Main, 29 March 1971)

Time has marched on since Powell spoke these words. But in some respects they foreshadow the theme that he has developed on a more sophisticated plane in recent years. A 'new balance of power' in Europe is a much more likely prospect now than it was twenty years ago; and the argument still holds that a new grouping in Central Europe would be incompatible with the EEC as it is currently known. Powell is implying that if anything is to be 'obliterated' it is the 'new unification of Western Europe' rather than the other way round.

In the wake of such momentous events, the intricacies of 1992 become to look all too peripheral for serious comment. If it is no longer necessary for American forces to be stationed in Western Europe; if, to use Powell's terminology, 'the desirability of political and military unification of Europe west of the Iron Curtain line' has been swept away by the realization that Russia poses no threat and nuclear weapons pose no credible deterrent, then the debate is bound to take a significantly different turn.

The case for free trade in Europe will remain. To that extent, the arguments concerning harmonization, regulation, and the like will still be heard. It will, however, be a practical debate. It will once again be about the possibility of creating a genuine Common Market rather than an economic and monetary union.

Powell may or may not be correct in believing that the creation of a single market disguises far-reaching political intentions. If, however, for the sake of argument his premise is accepted, then it is these intentions which will be forced to adapt to the new balance of power that is envisaged, but which cannot yet be identified with any precision. The whole question adds further spice to Powell's assertion that 'there ain't gonna be no 1992'.

CHAPTER SEVEN

A VIEW FROM THE 'LEFT'

Britain's membership of the EEC would make sense if, but only if, we accepted the implications of complete absorption, economic and political, into the new continental state.

ENOCH POWELL

The referendum drew attention to the tendency of some Conservatives to regard the European Community as a potential bastion against socialism. This feeling – which is still widespread – is somewhat curious given the political composition of so many continental governments since the war. Nevertheless, it has been a widely held assumption that the type of economic programme traditionally favoured by the British Labour party would run counter to many of the rules of the European Community. As has already been argued in the first chapter, fear of the Labour party's left wing was strong enough to have been a potent factor in securing a Yes vote.

We have also seen how, for Powell, this whole approach is thoroughly objectionable. The suggestion that political parties or individuals might seek to wrong-foot their domestic opponents by using the institutions of the Community as an alternative to winning popular support at home is contrary, in Powell's opinion, to the central principle of parliamentary democracy. However bitterly opposed he may have been in the past to policies that imperil the economic freedom of individuals – for example, the closed shop – he has taken pains on a number of occasions to disassociate himself from attempts by similar-minded libertarians to appeal over the heads of the British courts and Parliament to Brussels or Strasbourg. To pursue such a course is totally irreconcilable with Powell's concept of the sovereignty of Parliament.

His attitude is well summed up by what he said in June 1973: 'Let no one dare to admit that he prefers to substitute the decisions of others for the decisions of his own people in case he might not like what his own people would decide.'

In fact, there are a number of people who are quite prepared to make such an admission; and who argue that justice for the individual is more important than the means by which it is obtained. Since, however, Powell challenges the whole concept of universal human rights it is not surprising that he gives this argument short shrift.

In any case, it is not just human rights that are at stake. Some of the policies that Conservatives have hoped to see outlawed by the Community are part of the daily battle of practical domestic politics. These may, in the opinion of some Conservative party members, be damaging and undesirable. But to suggest that they are incompatible with the Treaty of Rome is tantamount to saying that the right of the British electorate to choose an alternative economic programme is now denied them – unless the United Kingdom leaves the Community.

The superficial attractions of allowing foreign law to handicap one's political opponents may seem self-evident to those currently on the winning side. However, as time passes the extent of this superficiality becomes ever more apparent. 'Red-blooded socialism' – if it still exists outside certain sections of the British Labour party – might well find itself confronted by the Community's Commissioners and European Court; but that does not alter the fact that there are still plenty of possibilities for state intervention in the Community that are likely to be much more agreeable to Neil Kinnock than to Margaret Thatcher. Conservative confidence in the Treaty of Rome still rests upon the assumption that the Labour party's socialism is different in kind and in degree from 'left-wing' programmes on the continent. But this is a perception that Kinnock is now at pains to dispel; and he appears to be equally prepared – if his party will let him – to use every means, including the resources and the authority of the European Community, to promote his brand of socialism at home.

There is another element in Kinnock's conversion. It is the feeling – evident, although by no means unanimously shared, on both sides of the political divide – that Britain's economy is now inextricably bound up with those of the rest of the Community. At some stage in the future, so the argument goes, membership of the EMS is inevitable (this is shorthand for saying after Thatcher ceases to be Prime Minister); in order to compete with the United States and Japan, 'Europe' will have to 'play these countries at their own game, and beat them at it.'

If, the argument runs, this means state intervention, so be it. Politicians of all parties will be forced to accept that the role of the European Community is to ensure that European firms are at no disadvantage against their international competitors. European industry competing in Europe will accept no less. They will insist upon trading in a single European currency; and in time will demand of the EEC that it assumes all those characteristics of a single trading entity that individual countries, such as the United States and Japan, enjoy by definition. This whole argument is one that an increasing number of politicians finds compelling.

This thought is also behind the demands of certain leading European businessmen for a European Community industrial strategy, including direct government support, to help European companies overcome the problems that are expected to arise once the single market is fully in place . The fears prompting these demands are of a Europe overrun by foreign competitors, and particularly by the Japanese. For example, the managing director of Fiat, Cesare Romiti, was reported as saying at a conference organized by the European Parliament in early March 1989 that 'I myself refuse to consider the possibility of handing over the European market to the Japanese or to the Americans as inevitable.'

This analysis is shared by people on both sides of the political divide. They might disagree as to the measures which best serve this new trading bloc; but they would unite against those in both the Labour and the Conservative parties who argue that the United Kingdom can still have significant discretion in deciding her economic destiny. Instead, they see the realities of the global market as paramount, dictating the course that the EEC as a whole must follow.

Thus, the simple classifications of 'right' and 'left' are increasingly unhelpful in defining the parameters of the debate. Both sides of the political divide — and both sides of industry as well — are competing with one another to cultivate potential allies in Brussels for the policies they wish to see implemented both domestically and throughout the EEC.

It is therefore to be expected that there should be those who see potential prizes specifically for the Labour party in the creation of a single market; and indeed this is nothing new. There has always been a section of the Labour party that has regarded membership of the Community as helpful — indeed, perhaps even essential — for the advance of a certain kind of socialism. True, for a long time it seemed as if this was very much a minority view. The possibility of this now changing is particularly significant, given that it coincides with the first real signs of disquiet on the Conservative side as to what 1992 might mean in practice.

Before examining this development, however, it should be noted in passing that the Labour party's performance upon the EEC has been one of great disappointment and, perhaps, disillusionment to Powell. For a considerable period, he placed his trust in the Labour party to get Britain out of the EEC. Partly, this may have been born of wishful thinking; equally, there was the undoubted necessity, from Powell's point of view, of keeping the issue alive. Nevertheless, there is every indication that Powell had genuine faith in the Labour party's determination to reverse the decision to enter the Community; without this faith, he would have found it difficult to justify his assertion that a vote for Labour was the duty of all who shared his objective.

Given the Labour party's current attitude and past record, there may indeed be many who are glad that they did not take Powell's advice. This last point is not made in any spirit of cynicism or gloating. It is simply that Powell placed more faith in the Labour party than did many of his supporters, even though they acknowledged the superiority of his political knowledge and experience. Was it because they lacked his courage, or because they understood the Labour party better than he did? Whatever the reason, it could be argued that on this issue it is they who have been proved right.

Powell almost seems to have recognized this himself. In an article for the *Spectator* in October 1980, he posed the question, 'Who speaks for England now?' At that stage, he still had not lost his trust in the Labour party's determination to leave the Community. Having reminded his readers that 'The Labour party is never to be taken more seriously than when it looks as if it were destroying itself' he went on to argue that:

> Whoever leads the Labour party from now on will wear, whatever other armour or impedimenta he carries, the declared decision to recall to Britain and Britain's Parliament the exclusive control of the law, the taxation, and the policies of this United Kingdom. The more than two-thirds majority of the Labour party conference which took that decision reflected the more than two-thirds majority of the people of Britain who are likewise deter-

mined to recover what was being taken away from them in 1972. The nation has at last heard its own mind being spoken, in terms and in a manner that will admit of no recall.

(*Spectator*, 11 October 1980)

This is some distance away from how he considered the same aspect of the question eight years later:

> If the great issues of principle – of freedom, of rights, of power, of national defence – are no longer fought out where they were fought out formerly, in the national arena of parliamentary and political debate, can that be just the result of an exceptional coincidence of voluble but empty-headed non-entities?
>
> A suspicion lurks that will not be repressed. There is a doubt not far below the surface. Perhaps after all the people do not care? Perhaps it does not matter to them who will inhabit and control their country a generation hence? Perhaps it does not matter to them who sets their taxes or who makes their laws? Perhaps it does not matter to them if they are a pawn in the power game of others?
>
> If so, they will not need a genuine parliamentary opposition, an opposition of principle, and Neil Kinnock really has nothing more to do than try to find out how to out-Thatcher Thatcher.
>
> I do not want to believe this. I have tried not to believe it. But we are the prisoners of our own desires. It could be true after all.'

(Aldridge, 18 March 1988)

In other words, Powell has faced and answered the question posed above. '*I have tried not to believe it. But we are the prisoners of our own desires.*'

Powell had indeed tried very hard. Before the 1979 general election he had said:

> The situation of the two contending parties is not the same. In the cabinet, in the government, and in the present parliament the Labour party is divided. At the top it has fallen victim to its recurrent disease of Macdonaldism or wanting to dine out with duchesses; but its heart and its rank and file are solidly with majority opinion in the country. Labour in government again would be held on a

tight rein; Labour in opposition would shed its Macdonaldism overnight and come out all but one hundred per cent for the policy of its conference.   (Kent, 12 October 1978)

In October 1981, he warned the Conservative party that:

> All the indications now from whatever source are that opinion in the United Kingdom is preponderantly, and increasingly preponderantly, hostile to our membership of the Community. One section of the public after another has been made aware of the reality of the renunciation of self-government and of the impact on their lives and interests of the loss of national freedom.
>
> The Labour party and the trade-union movement are, in this respect at least, in unison with the majority of the electorate; and their commitment to withdrawal, unlike the commitment of 1974 to renegotiation, is the product of protracted deliberation and debate and drawn in terms as overt, specific, and binding as they could be made.   (Blackpool, 14 October 1981)

But, after Labour's second electoral defeat, Powell's confidence in the Labour party disappeared. Until 1983, Powell had spoken of, and confronted personally, the 'cruel dilemma between party allegiance and political belief on the one hand and the promptings of their natural patriotism upon the other.' But now:

> All this has been altered by the electoral and moral collapse of the Labour party and the despicable scenes which have followed that collapse. To watch them is like witnessing the commanders and officers of a routed army lead the headlong flight of their own troops, throwing down and trampling, as they do so, the very standards and ensigns under which they have taken the field.
>
> To abjure the policies and promises which they themselves so recently offered to the electorate is regarded by the second-raters, third-raters, and fifteenth-raters who aspire to lead the routed remnant of their party as the principal condition of success, thus presenting the edifying spectacle of politicians openly disclosing that they never sincerely meant or believed the things they said to the electorate a month or two before, when the electoral outcome was still unknown.

It is a scene fit to excite the pity as well as the disgust of the Labour party's bitterest and most prejudiced enemies. For those of us who believed and still believe that the Labour party represented an essential element in Parliament and the British body politic and who remember times when Labour 'spoke for England', the sight is more than pitiful: it is tragic.

One thing however has happened. It is not, as some foolish people declare, that the issue of Britain's parliamentary independence and sovereignty has been finally decided in the negative. The question has not been closed: it has been changed. It has ceased to be an issue between the Ins and the Outs, between Government and Opposition, Tories and Socialists. By one of those weird chances in which political history abounds, it has become de-politicized, in the sense of being divorced from every other issue of inter-party division. The cause is now everybody's and anybody's. Behind the complacent facade of conventional approval and obligatory cliche, patriotism has become permissible in high places.   (Eastbourne, 2 September 1983)

To some extent, Powell was correct in predicting that supporters of the Conservative party would become less timid in their reservations over the Community once this ceased to be associated with support for the Labour party. What he did not anticipate was that the Labour party would undergo a similar process, but in reverse; that just as the Conservative party began to wake up to what a practical loss of sovereignty could mean, the Labour party saw the chance of gaining European support for the domestic policies that Margaret Thatcher herself had rejected.

It seems now as if both parties are asking themselves whether the European Community is as inclined towards free enterprise as they had formerly either hoped or feared. Powell is obviously interested in the answer to this question. But it must be said that, for him, this is not the issue that matters.

I ought to have stuck to my first intention.

When, in 1972, the House of Commons, albeit by a whisker under the extremity of pressure, consented formally to renounce all those rights and liberties − the exclusive power to tax, make law, and call governments to account − which past generations had laboriously won, I decided it was no longer any place for me:

>*I would not outstay the last session of the independent Parliament of the United Kingdom, which would come to an end in October 1972.*
>
>My letter to the Chancellor of the Exchequer soliciting the Chiltern Hundreds was already in draft that August.

For various reasons, which Powell explained in this *Sunday Express* article, the letter was not sent. But there is every indication that this is something he regrets: 'I ought to have known. A House of Commons and a party which passed the European Communities Bill and the European Assembly Bill would stoop to lick any spittle.' The 'spittle' was the Anglo-Irish Agreement; and he asked: 'Can a House of Commons, can a nation which could swallow what Britain swallowed on November 15 [1985], ever regain freedom and self-respect? It is a question which only those with a blind faith in their own country and people as proof against ultimate despair can still answer with a yes' (*Sunday Express*, 1 December 1985).

As will be considered shortly, Powell believes that there are grounds for hope in the recent speeches of the Prime Minister that Britain is recovering the determination to have its own way. The remarkable thing is that the Labour party should be moving towards acceptance of the European Community at the very moment when Conservative unease is on the increase; and that by doing so, the Labour party is making it easier for the Conservative party to reoccupy, if it wishes, the ground that had been abandoned by Edward Heath.

Before examining this further, however – and for the sake of completeness – reference should be made to the centre parties. David Steel, for example, might have wished that he had paid more attention to these words of Powell in 1978, describing the political characteristics of the then Foreign Secretary, David Owen:

>The Foreign Secretary may not be a man after everybody's heart (who is?), but no one who has observed him since he reached that office can be in any doubt that Dr Owen is a man who looks far ahead.
>
>As one who has a career of some thirty years in human probability ahead of him, he takes the long view, and is determined not to be so deeply committed to current policies, trends, and assumptions that he would be prevented in years to come from espousing any cause which then seemed likely to carry him to the top.
>
>(Southborough, 12 October 1978)

In other words, Dr Owen is a man who likes to keep his political options open. What prompted this observation was the statement by Dr Owen that 'It may well be that the British people and this Parliament, as they have every right constitutionally to do, may wish to reassess the question of British membership [of the European Community]. That is open to them at any time, but I believe that to do so after such a short period would be little short of disastrous.' Powell interpreted this as a readiness by Dr Owen to jettison his support for membership should this become electorally expedient.

But of course this was before the formation of what came to be known as the SDP. This party represented something different:

> Once the Labour party was committed unambiguously to taking Britain out of the Market, it ceased to be habitable to that little coterie of Labour members dedicated to the ambition of seeing Britain a province in a new West European state. The creation of the Social Democratic Party, with all the new lines of fissure which it hopes and threatens to create in British politics, has nothing to do with moderation – why is it 'moderate' to wish to live under laws not made by Parliament? – nor with a wistful preference for economic and financial policies already proved disastrous under Wilson and Heath.
>
> If you want to know what the SDP is about, look at its morning star, Roy Jenkins, the greatest Euro-bureaucrat of them all, a man who would never put up with anything British if he could find something foreign to embrace instead. The SDP is the extreme pro-European party, whose one common characteristic and undisputed stance is devotion to the destruction of Britain's parliamentary independence. Anyone who thinks that a bit rough should be aware that one of the SDP's proposals is to take away even the scrutiny, let alone the control, of European legislation from the House of Commons and give it to the Assembly at Stras-bourg.   (Gloucester, 30 September 1981)

This, incidentally, would suit the nationalists too. The more that power is transferred from Westminster to Brussels, the stronger the case for regional parliaments in Scotland and Wales. If Scottish or Welsh independence returns to the political agenda in any real sense, the European dimension will be much more important than on the last occasion. The House of

Commons will have to fight hard if it is not to be perceived as dispensable.

The immediate issue, however, is the effect of 1992 upon the attitudes of the two major parties towards the EEC. A turning point for both seems to have been the appearance of the Commission's President, Jacques Delors, at the 1988 Trade Union Conference. His presence on such a platform raised some eyebrows in Britain, given the tradition of political neutrality in which the British civil service is nurtured. It seems, however, as if this could be another example of the way British customs are so often out of step with Community practice. Since his TUC speech, Delors has gone on to make a personal appearance at the launch of the European Socialist Group's manifesto for the 1989 European elections. And Commissioner Leon Brittan was seen to be campaigning for the Conservative party candidate in the by-election at Richmond in February 1989.

Of greater importance than the fact of his appearance is what Delors told the TUC Conference. He argued that trade unions throughout Europe should demand 'social' policies to counterbalance the economic effects of a single market – like, for example, regional aid policies and a programme for workers' rights. As he explained, 'It would be unacceptable for Europe to become a source of social regression, while we are trying to rediscover together the road to prosperity and employment.'

Powell has admitted the regional problem arising from the single market; but not the solution proposed by Delors. For Powell, the problem is inherent in the type of economic community implied by 1992.

> We are familiar, classically familiar, in Britain with what is called the problem of the regions. The conditions of free trade, identical currency, unimpeded movement, and the rest which exist inside a unitary state such as ours result in the concentration of industry and population in the economically favourable areas, and this concentration in turn can set up a vicious circle of decline in the areas that are peripheral.
>
> I mentioned concentration 'of population' as well as of economic activity; and of course large shifts of population did and still do take place within the national territory. Nevertheless, even where these shifts encounter no political or cultural obstacles, they still encounter frictional resistance from deep and physical causes. Hence severe actual impoverishment as well as severe depopulation often occur simultaneously when these centripetal economic forces are operating.

If this is the picture inside a nation, and inside a nation as relatively homogeneous as Britain has until recently been and a nation as historically centralized as Britain, how much severer must be the effect when an island nation becomes peripheral to a new economic area, embracing both it and the adjacent land mass, under a system of internal free trade coupled with an external policy of autarky and trade restriction.

The consequences in this case are immensely sharpened because, though movement of labour within the area may be theoretically and legally as unimpeded as that of goods, it is in practice inhibited by linguistic, cultural, political, and other barriers, so that the economic safety valve of mobility of labour, which the theory of a common market implies and assumes, does not in practice operate.

This is the predicament in which Britain has been placed by inclusion within the EEC – of being in effect in relation to Europe one single depressed region like the Northeast or Ulster in relation to the United Kingdom. It is one of history's most mocking ironies that the German customs union, which set out to dominate Europe and conquer Britain in the form of Bismarckian or Hitlerian military force, has at last vanquished the victor by drawing Britain into a *Zollverein* which comprises Western Europe and aspires to comprise the Mediterranean as well. If the ghosts of the Hohenzollerns come back to haunt this planet, they must find a lot to laugh at.

(Grimsby, 20 May 1977)

The regional problem is often seen as a 'Labour party' issue. It is, therefore, of some interest that Powell should not have dismissed it as an issue of concern only to those who lack faith in market forces and in the inherent tendency of the economy to overcome its own imbalances and imperfections.

There is surprisingly another issue of common ground between Powell and the Labour party – namely, the balance of trade between the United Kingdom and the rest of the Community. The word 'surprisingly' is justified, because many of Powell's economic speeches in the past have been exhortations to allow the pound to float, and have argued that the so-called balance-of-payments crisis is no crisis at all. Powell has often asserted that there is nothing naturally 'good' about exports or 'bad' about imports: and therefore, although the vast trade gap between Britain and the Community is a problem for those who have heralded the Community as a means of providing British exporters with a major new market for their goods, it was not necessarily an aspect of Community membership that Powell needed to explore himself. He could confidently have left this to the Labour party, given the passionate feelings it arouses within the Labour movement.

These feelings have been played upon further by strong hints from the Conservative government that they intend after 1992 to discontinue the practice of including EEC trade when calculating the monthly trade balance. The logic of this is understandable. If the EEC is to comprise a single market, there is no more justification for compiling trade figures between, say, France and England than there is between Yorkshire and Cornwall. This is what a single market is about; and this is what the Foreign Office Minister, Lynda Chalker, presumably meant when she told a business gathering in Glasgow in October 1988 that imports into Britain from EEC countries should not be called imports after 1992.

It has not been lost on the Labour party that this provides a means of removing 'at a stroke' some twelve billion pounds from the United Kingdom's annual deficit in trade in manufactured goods. Bryan Gould, the Labour party's spokesman on Trade and Industry, has already asked for an assurance that trade statistics after 1992 will be compiled upon the same basis as before. His request was prompted by remarks from another government minister, Alan Clark, who said in answer to questions in the House of Commons on 15 February 1989 that 'After 1992 the imbalances in that form will no longer exist. There is a school of thought which argues that after 1992 and the completion of the internal market, deficits will disappear in that form and the imbalances will be simply regional and sectoral' (*Hansard*, c. 311).

As has already been hinted, Powell might have been expected to belong to this school of thought himself. This, however, may be a false assumption.

> The clearest symptom, if not instrument, of the economic subjugation of Britain is the huge non-oil trading deficit of the United Kingdom with the rest of the Community. This is one-way free trade with a vengeance.
>
> Of course, I understand perfectly well – and so do you – that any trading nation will have a deficit with one set of trading partners and a surplus with another: I am not talking the primeval language of barter or bilateral trade. I understand also that for con-

siderable periods a nation may have an overall trading deficit which is balanced by an inflow of invested capital. I understand finally – few better – that if governments interfere with the movement of the exchange rate, they can produce a howling artificial deficit and no endeavours on the part of their citizens can do anything to prevent it.

But all this has nothing to do with the meaning of our deficit with the EEC. Our deficit with the EEC is the result not of free trade but of restriction. It is the consequence for this nation of the internal free trade of the community combined with its external policy of control and exclusion, which forces us into an unnatural trading partnership with the continent while denying us our natural trade partnerships with the rest of the world, as a result of the Community's basic policy of self-sufficiency in food.

(Grimsby, 20 May 1977)

From this short extract, it can be seen that it is not so much the trade gap itself that is important to Powell, but the 'unnatural trading partnership' that it implies. Powell remains sceptical, however, of the conventional measurements of an economy's health, many of which are favoured by the Labour party and others who stake so much on Britain's place in economic 'league tables'.

The unreal dangers cluster round the popular concept of competitiveness, and the deductions drawn from Britain's supposed 'uncompetitiveness'. These range from dire predictions of national bankruptcy to threats of this country being 'unable to feed itself' or becoming 'de-industrialised'. Bankruptcy is of course a metaphor inapplicable to a nation such as ours, or indeed to any nation, unless it is in the position of Egypt or China in the 19th century, whereby the creditors of the country actually put in receivers by brute force and take over the collection of taxes and even the running of the country. We would do well, therefore, to forget notions of bankruptcy or insolvency and concentrate instead upon analysis of the alleged 'uncompetitiveness'.

Productivity comparisons

It appears that this means that more man hours, or whatever

measure of human effort is adopted, are required here to turn out a given quantum of certain goods or articles than in other countries, called 'competitor countries'. This has in fact been true of the comparison between Britain and the United States since the first half of the 19th century, when parliamentary investigators were actually sent across the Atlantic to find out how the Americans did it and why Britain was 'uncompetitive'. Though like is not always compared with like in these exercises of international comparison, I dare say that a very large number of genuine such cases could be produced today, ranging from France and Germany to Japan.

What is wrong is not so much the comparison of productivity as the deductions drawn from that comparison as to the commercial and economic consequences.

The outside world has continued to trade, and to trade to mutual advantage, with the United States despite the unfavourable ratios of respective productivity. The reason is two-fold. First, the superiority of the United States in productivity is not uniform: in some industries the gap between it and other countries is wider than in others. It therefore pays the Americans instead of producing everything themselves to concentrate upon the whole on those forms of production where their superiority is greatest and to 'farm out' (so to speak) to others the tasks where their lead is less, even though they could produce the goods in question more efficiently themselves if they set out to do so. The second reason runs concurrently with the first. The exchange rate between the dollar and other currencies stands at a level whereby, translated into dollar terms, the goods of which the production is 'farmed out' can be sold more cheaply in the United States than the corresponding home products.

The exchange rate

This point about the exchange rate ought not to need much elaboration at a time when British manufacturers and exporters are loudly complaining that the rise in the exchange rate of sterling has made their goods 'uncompetitive'. They do not of course mean that their own productivity – their man-hours per ton, or whatever – has fallen since the exchange rate of sterling rose. They are in fact declaring (though they do not seem to realize it) that the supposed link between productivity and competitiveness is nonsense.

The exchange rate contains the answer to the apparent paradox. If identical goods were being produced at widely differing efficiency in different parts of the United Kingdom or if the United Kingdom and Germany, or Japan, or the United States, were part of a single unit with a single currency, then of course the less efficient producers would be knocked out. That is why Germany is so keen for Britain to go into the European Monetary System, so that it can wipe out the British industries with which it is in competition.

But a customs union without a common currency — or, put it another way, free trade combined with a free exchange rate — enables production to be carried advantageously on in different countries at different, perhaps widely different, levels of efficiency. When the Lancashire cotton manufacturers demanded at the end of the last century to be protected against Bombay, it was not Indian efficiency that frightened them but the exchange rate of the rupee.

Of course, the standard of living, so far as that is measurable in terms of productivity (a very important and far-reaching qualification), will be relatively lower in Britain, or rise more slowly in Britain, than in countries where productivity is higher or increasing faster. We never felt either surprised or outraged by the superior material affluence of the Americans. What we need not fear, however, so long as we remain a nation with our own currency and allow the exchange rate of that currency to move freely, is that our inferior productivity or our 'uncompetitiveness'(if we are silly enough to describe it so) will drive us out of international trade, or impoverish us, or de-industrialize us, or leave us without the means to import food. All these are bogies to be relegated to the world of Hans Andersen.

If these are not the real dangers, what are? You may be surprised if I say that they are social and political rather than economic or, more precisely, economic in their form but social and political in their nature. I will classify them under two rubrics — inflation, and the loss of economic independence.'

And upon the second of these, Powell said the following:

It was said after the Second World War that Britain had lost an empire and failed to find a role. I am prepared to say that since 1972 Britain has ceased to be nation and failed to become a province. Britain's membership of the EEC would make sense if, but only if, we accepted the implications of complete absorption, economic and political, into the new continental state. We should then be a region, with all the advantages and disadvantages, such as those accepted by Wales or Ulster as part of the United Kingdom.

Continental system of trading

Since, however, predictably and ineluctably, we are not prepared to be a province but continue to behave as if we were a nation, the economic consequences are disastrous and must become progressively more so. We are forced into a pattern of trading which fits well the continental system of maximum self-sufficiency and high-cost agriculture but bears no relation to the British economy. We are deprived of control of our national assets in agriculture and fisheries and, increasingly, in disposal of our sources of energy. We have exchanged our external commercial autonomy for a common policy, in forming which we can never have more than a small minority voice – often a minority of one. On top of all the rest, we are a net contributor to the rest of the Community – visibly in the form of our growing net payment, invisibly in the price and trade disadvantages inherent for us in membership.

Social self-consciousness

There is, besides, something else, intangible and unprovable but nonetheless a reality and the greatest reality. Economic performance is connected with social self-consciousness. Men and women in real life do not work and produce as selfish, autonomous, atomic units. They give the best of which they are capable only under the pressure and inspiration of a sense of identity – of the answer to Churchill's historic question 'What sort of people do they think we are?'

    We cannot give a satisfying response to that question or, consequently, to our economic environment, so long as we have been told that the answer is: 'You are no longer a nation and you must hurry up and become a European province.' Unmistakably, the crisis point is approaching when that conflict, hitherto suppressed and subconscious, becomes open and conscious. The celebrated 'decline of Britain', which is far more subjective than objective, is unstoppable until that crisis has been reached and resolved.

(London, 21 March 1980)

What divides Powell from his opponents is that they believe that Britain can only compete internationally, and particularly with Japan, by becoming a European province. The above speech is of interest because it dismisses all such fears as groundless. For Powell, the economic analysis is at fault; and therefore the assumptions upon which the Community's case rests are fundamentally flawed also.

Powell does accept, however, that *'Britain's membership of the EEC would make sense'* if the political will existed to accept all the implications of being part of a new continental state. In other words, it may be conceded that a country like the United States has inherent trading and economic advantages in comprising a homogeneous nation with a vast home market and its own single currency and government; but if the EEC wants those advantages for itself, the only way they can be obtained is for the EEC to become a homogeneous nation itself. For Powell, that is almost the equivalent of saying to an individual that he must become a completely different person and renounce the past that has made him what he is; Powell contends that this is neither possible, desirable, nor necessary.

There are, however, some who are ready to accept these implications; and believe they are right to do so, given the forces of competition that European countries would face once the Community ceased to exist. Of these competitive forces, Japan is often regarded as the most serious.

I do not know whether the politics of our trade relationship with Japan are more humiliating or absurd. I should, strictly speaking, say the EEC's trade-relationship with Japan, because of course as a member of the EEC the United Kingdom no longer has any trade policy of its own, though we are sometimes allowed to go off by ourselves to Tokyo or Timbuktu and indulge in antics which would suggest to the untutored that we are still an independent nation. However, whether it is *our* trade relationship or the EEC's trade relationship, the question remains the same: more humiliating or more absurd? The answer, I think, is that it is humiliating *because* it is absurd.

Japan, it appears, has a huge current-account surplus. It seems that in the fiscal year 1977–78, just closed, that surplus was thirteen billion dollars, and still on the up-and-up. Well then; Japan must have had a capital-account deficit of thirteen billion dollars last year and rising still. Japan is lending to the rest of the world at a huge rate; for every overall surplus on current account is balanced by an exactly equal deficit on capital account. That happens to be how God created the world. If the Japanese like to lend all this capital, what, it may be asked, is wrong with that?

Japanese investment

Personally I have no objection to Japanese capital being invested in British industry. As the Emperor Vespasian remarked, in a slightly different context, 'it doesn't smell'. And they can't take it away again; at least we never managed to get the railways and tramlines and electric power stations back from Argentina, and little good they would have done us if we had.

However, it may be said that it isn't in British industry that the Japanese are investing: either they are investing in the industries of other countries or else they are just advancing consumer credit and enabling their customers to live 'on tick'. Neither of these objections is valid. If Japan has a current surplus with Britain but is not lending to Britain, then somebody else must be lending to Britain instead to make up for it: the outflow of capital from Japan, which balances Japan's global current surplus, must come to rest somewhere in the world, directly or indirectly. If, on the other hand, Japan hasn't a current surplus with Britain, what are we fussing about anyhow?

As for the objection that Japan is lending to Britain for consumption and not investing in British industrial capital, there are two alternative answers: first, if the British government likes to run up debt to fund its current expenditures, that must be our fault and not something for which we should blame the Japanese; but secondly, the Japanese are not so dumb as to lend their capital without the prospect of a good return on it – in other words, somewhere or other they will see that it gets invested productively.

Japanese imports

Still, the plain man thinks to himself: Japan's current-account surplus consists partly of those sales of motor cars which we should
otherwise be employed making and selling to ourselves. Hence the
demand to prohibit or penalize imports from Japan or to persuade
the Japanese by threats or cajolery – and neither seems to be
working very well – to stop their own car manufacturers from
making and selling abroad so many cars.

In days gone by, when the pound was exchangeable for a
fixed quantity of gold, there would have been a good deal of sense
in this demand, because then the balance of payments was main-
tained by actually reducing the amount of money – deflation, for
short – in the country which was tending to have a deficit on its
current account. The current account surplus of Japan would then
have been balanced not only by Japanese lending but by actual
deflation – or depression – in the importing countries.

In these enlightened times, thanks to floating exchange rates,
that does not happen: the slightest sign of a country's propensity
to export outstripping its propensity to lend or invest abroad is in-
stantly corrected by an upward movement of the exchange rate of
its currency, which restores the balance again.

International trade

Now, it is quite true that if more of our cars are bought from Japan
and fewer made by ourselves, we shall have to switch, to that
extent, from car-making to making something else, but with the
sure knowledge that that something else is a more valuable application of our effort than making cars. This after all, is the whole
story of international trade – nay, of trade itself – as an instrument
of economic progress: to buy from others, or import from elsewhere, in order to free one's time and talents for doing something
more worthwhile. Do not ask: what *is* that something else? The
money spent upon an imported Japanese car has changed hands,
but it has not evaporated or left these shores: in the hands of its
new owners it is already seeking, has probably already found, that
something else.

Let me add, too, that even if the new owner of the sterling

spends it on (say) a Grand National horse or racecourse, that is not the end of the matter, because the vendor of the existing asset, or some subsequent ultimate vendor, is not going to lay out the proceeds in demanding current production.

Dew from Heaven

I referred just now to these more enlightened times of floating exchange rates. I confess I was consciously anticipating; for, as so often in the past, mankind's comprehension generally has been slow to catch up with the beneficence of the instruments that have been placed at its disposal.

The reason for these humiliating and ridiculous Western embassies to the Mikado, begging him not to accumulate so large a current-account surplus on his balance of payments, is the general reluctance of governments the world over to allow the exchange rate to bestow its blessing like the dew from Heaven. The Mikado wants to keep the exchange rate of the yen down; the President of the United States and the European 'snake'-charmers want to keep the exchange rate of their respective currencies up. If something is amiss in Japan's trading relations with the rest of the world, it is that the yen is artificially under-valued and the other currencies correspondingly artificially over-valued in relation to one another. Who keeps it that way? Why, the very governments which are making all the bother.

Inferiority complex

It is absurd, yes; but it is also humiliating, and not just because all wilful absurdity is humiliating. We feel that the supposed success of Japanese exports and their so-called 'penetration' of the British home market is somehow a sign that there is something wrong with us: it is usually described as British industry being 'uncompetitive'. This gives us a terrible inferiority complex. Consequently, when we take part in these silly embassies to Tokyo, instead of treating the whole thing as a lark – a mutual game of log rolling whereby the nations help one another to fudge their own exchange rates to no good purpose – we feel that we have suffered a catastrophic loss of face before the triumphantly apologetic oriental.

'Cap in hand', that's the phrase; we are going 'cap in hand', we think, to the Japanese to beg them to protect us from some of the more extreme consequences of our own inefficiency. The true humiliation is in our fevered imagination; and it is none the less agonizing and damaging for being a form of self-punishment.

Why should we go on doing it? As in the past we have been able to bid the world defiance from behind the watery frontiers of our seagirt islands, trading at will but safe from harm, so today the liquid bulwark of the floating pound affords us automatic protection against even the most horribly efficient of our neighbours: their efforts can only enrich us, if we will leave things alone and not interfere. But if the politicians find the latent Luddism which is everywhere present too strong to defy, then at least it will be better for our ego — though not devoid of economic disadvantage — to slap a protective tariff on this or that class of beastly foreign articles, so that we can enjoy our own dearer and inferior products undisturbed.

Don't get me wrong; I'm not recommending such a course. Dear me, no; but to invert the famous words of a City gent twenty years ago: 'it doesn't make sense but it's patriotic' — far better, anyhow, than begging the Japanese to keep their goods at home.

Oh, but I forgot! I forgot, what I myself reminded you of at the start, that we don't have a trading policy of our own since 1973 and are not allowed by the EEC to do any such thing off our own bat. So all I can do, is to send a copy of this speech with my compliments to our lord and master Commissioner Haferkamp, who won't understand a word of it. Never mind; have patience. There is a fashion in all things, and no form of human folly lasts for ever.   (Basingstoke, 7 April 1978)

It is of interest, given this speech, to recall the words of Vice President Haferkamp while on a visit to Tokyo in May 1977:

Here I must be very frank. In the past there does seem to have been an inbuilt resistance in the Japanese economy to large-scale imports of products that compete directly with the products of Japanese industry. The open world trading system, to which we are all committed, implies acceptance of a growing interdependence between the industrialized countries. Yet unlike the other industrialized countries, imports of industrial goods into Japan only amount to twenty per cent as opposed to more than fifty per cent in the case of the European countries. However, I am glad to say after my talks at the Keidanren, that there does now seem to be a genuinely more open attitude to imports on the part of Japanese business.

To conclude, the present situation cannot be changed overnight, but I am convinced that it is in the mutual interests of the Community and Japan that we should achieve a better balance in our mutual trade. I am also convinced that protectionist measures are not the solution. With good will we should be able to find satisfactory solutions to our present difficulties since we both want the same thing: to preserve free trade.

The dichotomy between Powell's and the more fashionable approach could not be better illustrated than by comparing that statement with the foregoing speech.

The position of the Labour party upon this aspect of the question, however, is not easily summarized. It might agree with Powell that the United Kingdom no longer has a trading policy of its own. It might also regret the fact. But Labour politicians have not been renowned for their attachment to free trade in the past; many in fact have been as xenophobic as it is possible to be when it comes to foreign investment. It is doubtful, therefore, whether Powell's theory of international trade – and the extent to which it conflicts with the principles of 1992 – strikes much of a chord with the Labour party in this specific area.

But there is some common ground. As we have seen, Powell does not dispute that 1992 will exacerbate the problems of the regions; he also believes that Community membership is disruptive to the pattern of trade that most favours British interests.

The biggest disagreement between him and the Labour party arises when the solutions to these problems are discussed. The significant development to consider is the Labour party's apparent willingness to embrace the concept of what is known as 'social Europe' and which, according to Delors, is needed 'if working people are not to see the internal market as something of interest only to businessmen and entrepreneurs'.

If one takes Britain's regional problem as an example, it is clearly Powell's view that the disadvantage that parts of the United Kingdom will suffer as a result of the single market is deeply embedded in the 1992 structure, and cannot be overcome by what he would regard as the palliative measures proposed by the Commission to help the EEC's depressed areas.

In any case, no believer in market forces can believe, without inherent contradiction, that the expenditure of billions of pounds in Europe to aid backward regions will be any more successful than it was in the United Kingdom before Margaret Thatcher abandoned such an approach. On the other hand, one can see why the Labour party — whose enthusiasm for a regional policy continues unabated — should welcome the Delors strategy.

Powell would also gain some ironic pleasure from the singling out by Delors of 'businessmen and entrepreneurs' as the main beneficiaries of a single market. This was always the assumption, it is true, until organizations like the Institute of Directors began to appreciate how other, less business-friendly, considerations might be involved. It took until February 1989 for its Director General, then Sir John Hoskyns, to ask 'If the governments of other member states find free trade and capitalism so unpalatable, why did they adopt the 1992 programme? If the differing political colours of member-state governments necessitate such economically damaging compromises, how on earth can M. Delors seriously imagine that we can move to complete political and economic integration?'

One of the difficulties for the business community is that in lining up so strongly in favour of Britain's membership of the Community — and in helping to finance the case for doing so — it has become victim to the very vested interests which it has helped to create. As Powell has remarked, 'The institutions of the EEC create an ever-spreading vested interest on the part of those who service them, to whom this becomes a livelihood and a way of life.' He went on to give an example:

> Quite apart from politicians, there is the multitude of lobbyists, purporting to represent almost every interest with which the Common Market might interfere, who have thus gained an illimitable extension to the parasitical profession of go-betweens and know-somebody-who-knows-somebody else.
>
> (Westminster, 27 February 1982)

Or again:

> The political commitment was reinforced by the great corporate voices, the National Farmers' Unions and the Confederation of British Industry. For all in politics and quasi-politics, there is no

ball-and-chain to compare in weight and strength with past commitment, breakable (admittedly) if and when daddy (or, as the case
may be, mummy) turns. But all the daddies and mummies have
been wearing the same ironmongery for the same reasons.

There were vested interests of a more tangible nature. From
the moment of British membership, if not before, a new bureaucracy grew up, public and private, to handle relations with those in
the new seats of power at Brussels. Those thus engaged become
advocates of the indispensability of the institution with which
they operate, especially as their activities, in common with most
political activities on the continent, tend to be lushly remunerative.

(Cheam, 10 October 1984)

Sir John Hoskyns went even further when he said that 'There are signs that
the Brussels machine is becoming corrupted both intellectually and fin-
ancially ... Members of Parliament, officials, Commissioners, are all professional Europeans. They have all hitched their wagons to the European star.
Their careers, reputations, salaries, and pensions depend upon it. The professional European spends virtually all his waking hours with fellow Euro-
people. He can easily become alienated from his own countrymen unless
they unquestioningly accept his European vision.'

The vehemence of this language is accounted for by a growing fear in
the business community that 1992 is not all that it seems. To give but one
example, there is a list of items − by no means exhaustive − which are, in
one way or another, all on the EEC's agenda for securing 'social cohesion'
throughout the Community: they include framework directives on working
time and work organization; equal opportunity; parental leave; standard
employment laws and social-insurance schemes; workers' rights when
engaged and dismissed; a framework directive for informing and consulting
employees at community level; and the proposed European company
statute which, in the words of the Commission, 'will offer a number of
models for worker participation in the management of firms opting for that
legal form.'

The ambassador of the Federal Republic of Germany, Baron von Richt-
hofen reinforced the message when he told the Institute of Directors on 28
February 1989 that 'we should work as far as possible and practicable for
parity in social-security and social benefits, in occupational safety require-
ments, vocational training, and last but not least in the field of workers'
participation.'

As was argued in a report commissioned by the British Labour Group of Euro-MPs: 'One of the conclusions of this study is that the main virtue of the internal market measures is that it makes it easier for national governments to take accompanying measures. It therefore tends to support those who see the need for strengthening democratic state action. For socialists it is important that the internal market measures do not weaken the role of the state in the economy, and that 1992 is an opportunity for strengthening them.'

This is also behind the implied – if not outright – support that Neil Kinnock gave to the EEC socialist manifesto for the 1989 elections to the European Parliament, in which the case for political unification, more democratic accountability, and the social dimension was uncompromisingly advanced.

In this as in so much else, however, the Labour party's position was not without its internal detractors. In the House of Commons, Tony Benn explained that one view of Europe 'is that of a social Europe, linked to federalism and a European union. That view emerges in the Euro-manifesto, which was adhered to very recently – with reservations – by the Labour delegation. A reading of the manifesto leaves us in no doubt that the Labour delegation wants a federal union in Europe.'

However, this position is apparently to be distinguished from the British Labour party's view, which, according again to Benn, 'is difficult for anyone to identify correctly'. Nevertheless, as he explained: 'The Labour party conference has always been hostile to the Common Market. It fought for the referendum. [Edward Heath] signed the treaty of accession without it even being published, and we did not know what he had signed until he had signed it. He signed it under the prerogative; we said that we would have a referendum, and the vote went against us. At various times the party of which I am proud to be a member has favoured the repeal of section 2 of the European Communities Act, as the House must know very well. Whatever may be the result of our present policy reviews there is a total lack of enthusiasm for the sort of Europe spoken of by some in my party and the Conservative party. I suspect that, as the [Euro] election approaches, that European Social Democratic manifesto will not feature very much in our campaign' (*Hansard*, 23 February 1989 c. 1190–91).

More brutally still, Benn went on: 'People say that if we work for the Single European Act, women will get their rights, the water will be purer, and training will be better. That is rubbish. It is part of the attempt to consolidate the EEC' (*Hansard*, 23 February 1989 c. 1192). And so said Powell two years earlier:

The deliberate development of the European Economic Community into a political state is now not merely visible but no longer sedulously concealed. Freedom of trade, intercourse, and investment between nations is compatible with diversity of national laws and fiscal systems. The Community on the contrary asserts with increasing rigour the doctrine that trade can only be genuinely free between those who live under the same laws, have the same systems and levels of taxation, and use the same currency.

The doctrine is false. It equates international trade with the relations between citizens living in a unitary state. Under this doctrine harmonization becomes the instrument of amalgamation, of the elimination of sovereign states to form a new political unit. Its logical consequence is that within that new unit laws must be made and government carried on by a single central authority.

The doctrine of harmonization is incompatible, and was always intended to be incompatible, with sovereign British institutions. The writing showed up on the wall already when harmonization was extended beyond the removal of discriminatory barriers against trade into areas of purely domestic and internal concern. The levels of purity of bathing beaches or drinking water do not need to be harmonized in order that French people may spend holidays in Cleethorpes or English people in Cannes. It is no restraint of trade to be obliged to observe the standards of safety or quality which a state sees fit to insist upon for articles sold within its jurisdiction.

For a long time now the vast and growing volume of European Community legislation which harmonizes for harmonization's sake has been shrugged off with innocent ridicule as a manifestation of rampant bureaucracy rather than of a consistent will to political power. Of late that innocence has begun to be breached.   (Blackpool, 8 October 1987)

In this passage, Powell places himself in fundamental opposition to everything that 1992 stands for. He is not capable, however, of finding a solution to the Labour party's inconsistencies. Neil Kinnock has expressed strong reservations over the ability of British industry to withstand the extra competition that he expects from a single market. But he is aware also that across much of Europe, to quote the political commentator, Hugo Young, of the *Guardian*, 'a version of socialism rather than Thatcherism is the reigning orthodoxy'. It is becoming clear to business and the Labour party alike that the price to be paid for an expanded market need not — and probably won't be — Thatcherite in character. If business had understood the analysis propounded by Powell over the past twenty years, it would not now be so surprised.

The great disillusionment for Powell, however, is that this realization is now making it easier for Kinnock to honour one of his earliest policy commitments — that Labour should cease to be the anti-European party. Although there is still much about the European Community that is distasteful to socialism, it is clear that Kinnock sees party political advantages in moving closer to the socialist parties in Europe.

Powell, therefore, is faced with the spectacle of each of the major political parties turning a somersault in opposite directions in its relations with the European Community. He would be forgiven for wondering whether he is really alone in deprecating the fact that the party political interests of both parties are now seen to hang upon who gains the upper hand at Brussels rather than at Westminster. He is also aware that his view — and perhaps Thatcher's too — is up against the conventional wisdom that Britain has no choice other than to accept willingly or unwillingly the direction in which the economies of Western Europe are heading.

CHAPTER EIGHT

THE ROAD TO BRUGES

The Conservative Party has always seen itself as a pragmatic party as well as a national party.

ENOCH POWELL

'One is scared to cheer, lest premature applause might upset the act.' So spoke Powell in the aftermath of the Prime Minister's speech in Bruges on 20 September 1988; his words reveal his hope that at last, and much later in the day than he ever imagined, the Conservative party is beginning to change its mind about the European Community.

It is not often that a politician makes a speech that transforms a nation's political agenda. It is an easier task for Prime Ministers than for anyone else – although Powell has ignited more than his fair share of verbal explosions on the political scene. Now, Margaret Thatcher has chosen Powell's supreme issue to do the same, and in language that – in part – could have been directly transcribed from the speeches he made upon the subject twenty years ago. Like these speeches, Thatcher's remarks at Bruges may not have been read as carefully as they deserve. But the interpretation that has been placed upon them – whether accurately or inaccurately – has had the effect of rejuvenating the EEC debate and of reopening questions hitherto left to politicians outside the Establishment to explore.

The principal question now is whether the speech's significance is justified in terms other than its perceptiveness. Has Thatcher said anything new? If so, does this reflect fresh thinking within Whitehall – and, in particular, within the Foreign Office? What were the pressures which led

Thatcher to speak as she did? Is it simply that the Prime Minister now has the confidence to say in the open what, in the past, have frequently been reported as her private beliefs? Or is it that events to do with the single market, the social dimension, and *perestroika* have all combined to produce a change of attitude in government that would survive even Thatcher's departure from Downing Street?

This last point is tied up with whether Thatcher speaks for herself on this issue, or for the whole of the Conservative Party. The Bruges speech can be added to the already long list of Prime Ministerial statements that her cabinet colleagues have greeted with less than enthusiasm when asked about it off the record. The day after the speech was made, the Press was full of reports of damage-limitation exercises aimed at calming the furore her speech had provoked in Brussels and elsewhere.

But another reaction was also evident. Certain political and national figures who had been conspicuous hitherto by their silence seemed prepared to use 'Bruges' as an excuse for saying what they had been suspected of believing for some time. Powell made the point a little more explicitly:

> The politicians and particularly the Conservative party, who had known all along what was going on, began to take note. 'There are votes at stake here', said they to themselves.
>
> Now very properly in a parliamentary democracy there is nothing which has such a galvanic effect on politicians as the prospect of winning or losing what the Leader of the Opposition is popularly supposed to call 'lotza votes'. So they said to themselves, 'Boys, this is where we jump!'
>
> (London, 2 November 1988)

For Powell, however, the reaction of the Conservative party is too serious to be joked about for long; on the contrary, it is one of the pivotal issues.

> Britain without a Tory party is like a man with one arm cut off or a giant blinded in one eye — it cannot act effectively, it cannot see properly to live its life.
>
> I do not need to be reminded that in a two-party state, the form to which a parliamentary monarchy necessarily reverts as its normal condition, the great parties are immensely diverse and kaleidoscopic coalitions. I do not need to be told that Conservative

and Tory are not synonymous, and that the Conservative party comprises political elements which are positively anti-Tory: Whig, Liberal, conservative with a small 'c', and so on.

What I am saying is that so long as the United Kingdom, or whatever is left over after devolution and separatism have done their worst, remains a nation at all, there has to be a party in the state which embodies the national consciousness, whose thinking expounds the philosophy of nation, and whose tongue speaks the language of nation. Around that central core can congregate the bearers of all manner of other aspirations and insights; but the core itself is indispensable.   (Liverpool, 17 November 1978)

The Conservative party has not yet shown any real sympathy for what lies behind Powell's words in the above passage. On the other hand, if one examines through Powell's eyes the development of Conservative thinking since the referendum, it is possible to identify the road to Bruges earlier than is popularly supposed. In particular, the scepticism with which Powell greeted Thatcher's pronouncements before and during the early years of her premiership is much less evident in his later speeches than at the beginning.

For example, it was twelve years before Bruges – in June 1977 – that Thatcher, as Leader of the Opposition, went on the record in a speech in Rome saying 'I do not believe that the nation states in Europe will wither away.' It is unlikely, although not impossible, that this remark was prompted by the following passage from a speech made by Powell exactly a week earlier; in any case, the breach between them is well illustrated by this extract, in which Powell describes 'as clinically as possible' from his 'detached but not indifferent viewpoint' one of the elements of the Conservative party's 'tragedy':

The most acute and urgent element in that 'tragedy' – for I will continue to use my word – is that the Conservative party is now on the opposite side to Britain, to Britain as an independent, self-governing, sovereign nation such as Iceland or Norway, for instance, or Zambia or Jamaica.

If the Conservative party had been unduly slow to recognize a relative diminution in Britain's wealth or power, or unduly stubborn in claiming that, if other nations can go their own way on their own responsibility, so will we, that would do nobody any harm at all; for that, after all, is part of what a conservative party is about.

But when the Conservative party proclaims as a matter of proud conviction that, so far as Britain is concerned, the day of the nation state is over and that the manifest destiny of this island's inhabitants is to belong to a West European state; when the Conservative party denounces its political opponents for being hesitant or divided over surrendering the right of the British Parliament to control Britain's affairs; when the Conservative party becomes the advocate of ever-faster absorption of Britain into a European amalgam – that is a national disaster because it leaves millions of British people, the very people for whom the Conservative party exists to speak, without a political voice or a political home.   (Swansea, 17 June 1977)

Powell personalized the issue once Margaret Thatcher had become Prime Minister:

There is a sense in which every elected Prime Minister, even the worst – and there have been some bad ones – is representative of the nation in its current condition. Baldwin and Neville Chamberlain were as representative of the British people as was Winston Churchill, arguably more so. However mysterious, devious, and aleatory the modes by which a particular individual becomes Prime Minister, he would not have arrived there unless he had been, in the sense in which I am speaking, representative.

When the nation's fears, foibles, and follies, are uppermost, the nation gets itself someone who, however peculiar in other respects, is in those respects typical. Likewise, when the tides are changing or conflicting, it will be the Prime Minister who dramatizes them in his own person, because through electorate, Parliament, and Cabinet the contending forces focus at that point.

To be or not to be?

It is as thus representative of a nation which is failing to resolve the Hamlet question of being or not being that Mrs Thatcher is also failing to resolve it, by answering it with both Yes and No. While on the one hand she purports and aspires to assert the principle of nationality and did indeed, up to the point of her rebuff in May [Thatcher had adopted an aggressive line with her Community partners on the subject of the UK budget contribution, but only managed to secure in May 1980 a temporary agreement limiting British contributions for two or three years while a permanent solution was sought], strike out a course in Europe which was only rational and intelligible on the assumption that Britain intended to take back the national and parliamentary sovereignty given up in 1972, on the other hand she is to be heard and seen saying and doing things that point to a deliberate and cheerful intention to accomplish the work begun by Edward Heath and render Britain's reduction to the status of a province irreversible.

I will give one example. Throughout the 'battle of the Budget' – or should it be the 'battle of the £1000 million'? – the most explicit declarations were made that there would be no package deal, that the matter of Britain's net contribution being reduced to zero, or as near as possible, would be settled without reference to other questions and without conditions.

When the compromise agreement was arrived at eventually behind the Prime Minister's back and reluctantly acquiesced in by her, the House of Commons was solemnly assured that there was no package and that all other matters arising between Britain and the EEC would be dealt with separately and on their own merits. Now we have the Prime Minister going over to see the French President, publicly referring to the agreement as a package and averring that Britain would not 'break her promises'.

How to escape

There are, of course, explanations and excuses for this contradiction and ambiguity. 'Margaret,' say the apologists, 'has never been a committed "European", but she has to play the hand cautiously'. That is true, up to a point. The Cabinet and the parliamentary party is heavily populated with politicians who spent the last eight years, once they saw the way the wind blew, mouthing the anti-national slogans of 'European unity' and 'the European idea'. What is more, Mrs Thatcher herself went along with it all as a Cabinet minister, albeit home-oriented, and mouthed the slogan with the best. That is no doubt very awkward; for no operation is more painful and difficult, and the more so the higher up one is in the career structure, than 'getting off the hook'. But that is no excuse for acting as if the problem could be solved by the ambiguities of contradictory policies or of conflicting words and actions.

The nation as a whole is caught in the same embarrassment. It has to get out of it; for otherwise the question, to be or not to be, will be decided by default and decided against it. If the renunciation of nationhood performed in 1972 was an aberration, it must be recognized as such openly and honourably by the nation, and that act has to be performed on its behalf, not vicariously but representatively, by the Prime Minister. So far she has failed, whether from a failure of will, of conviction, or of analysis. In this the responsibility must be accepted, and the deficiency supplied, by the people at large; for the cause is that of the British people itself.

(Eastbourne, 30 September 1980)

The personality of Margaret Thatcher was an increasingly important feature of Powell's general argument once it became clear that her premiership was destined to be remarkable.

British politics is very much about persons. I refer to the fact that the dominating position and relative permanence of our Prime Ministers, combined with the public exposure which our parliamentary system enforces, results in most periods in politics taking a decided colour from the personality of the head of government. There is no need to be apologetic about this – much the contrary. Heroic epochs in our history are 'the days of Mr Pitt' and 'the days of Mr Churchill', in quite another sense from that in which the peaks of French history are associated with, for instance, Louis XIV or Napoleon I or de Gaulle.

There is, I fancy, no doubt about the identity of the person from whom these present years in politics take their colouring. Margaret Thatcher, for millions of British people, stands for something that they have hitherto not recently known – not, at least, for a quarter of a century. They see at the head of affairs somebody who personifies for them some of what they believe to be the political virtues. These are courage and directness. The fact that the qualities are represented – unprecedentedly at the summit of politics – by a woman only serves to intensify the impression and endue them with a certain panache. If these seem sometimes to be tinged with a certain simplicity of approach and naïveté of vision, people are not disposed to think the worse of them for that.

In a parliamentary democracy the public are prone to look for a representative in the Queen's chief minister, a representative not in the electoral or psephological sense but in the symbolical sense. They are looking for an expression in personal terms of what they think about themselves and their country, and an opportunity to believe that it can be brought a little closer to reality from the unattainable regions of myth and imagination. Courage and direct sincerity are certainly important ingredients in the alchemy of that representative achievement.

Still a nation?

And yet, and yet ... those who most ardently look for its accomplishment are filled with the anxiety, which does not diminish as the months pass by, that somehow it is going to elude us. They ask what is wanting; and I am going to attempt, despite the difficulty of definition, to frame my own answer to that question. I do not do so in the character of critic or ill-wisher: I do so because I too would wish to see fulfilled what I believe is the desire, unformulated or half-formulated, of my fellow countrymen.

If I could sum that desire up in a single word, the word would be 'nation': people want to be free of the growing sense that they are being progressively deprived, not just of the pride, but of the substance of being a nation; and looking around them in the world, they feel downgraded and passed by. Up to a point the words and mood which express this desire are provided by the Prime Minister. People, hearing her, are convinced that she shares the same frustration and nurtures the same ambition. They are then bewildered to find that the role implicit in those words and that mood is not acted out. If we, and they, can understand why, for all the evident courage and sincerity, the words and the mood are always in the end belied by the event, we shall be on the way to find the answer to our question.

Double standards

I believe we shall do so if at first we remain in the realm of words –

which after all are, in politics, not the opposite to actions, but the very stuff of actions. How comes it that Mrs Thatcher, after stoutly proclaiming in the face of Western Europe the national demands of Britain, is afterwards, or even simultaneously, heard indulging the full rhetoric of European integration and political unification? How comes it that when she has asserted her pride and confidence in Britain's material capability, her discourse then turns so easily into denunciation of whole classes of British society and of the British economy as 'uncompetitive'? How comes it, to look in another direction, that Mrs Thatcher, who has associated herself, no doubt with full conviction, to be 'rock hard for the Union' [of Great Britain and Northern Ireland], is able to place her signature beside that of the Union's bitterest enemy to statements perilously near to questioning it?

I find a common feature in all these – and other – bewilderments. It is the failure to realize, emotionally and intellectually, that an indispensable and unnegotiable element of nation is independence, and that the instinct for independence is in the British the underpinning of their national identity. Once this key is inserted, it fits all the locks. It is not possible for the British both to be a nation and also to have surrendered – to external authorities – the exclusive right of its Parliament to make laws and levy taxes and of the Queen's courts to interpret its laws and dispense justice. If its nationhood is asserted, that surrender must be recalled. If that surrender is not recalled, the assertion of nationhood is empty bluster.   (Southend, 24 April 1981)

The passage quoted immediately above asserts that 'the role' and 'the mood' implicit in Margaret Thatcher's words are *'not acted out ... the words and the mood are always belied by the event'*. If this is a fair criticism, it is one that might also be directed at the Bruges speech.

These words, however, were spoken before the Falklands War and before Powell was moved to applaud publicly Thatcher's political courage and perseverance. Referring to her reputation as the 'Iron Lady', Powell said the following words in the House of Commons following the Argentinian surrender:

Is the right hon. Lady aware that the report has now been received from the public analyst on a certain substance [i.e. iron] recently subjected to analysis and that I have obtained a copy of the report? It shows that the substance under test consisted of ferrous matter of the highest quality, that it is of exceptional tensile strength, is highly resistant to wear and tear and to stress, and may be used with advantage for all national purposes?

(*Hansard*, 17 June 1982 c. 1082)

This must rank as one of the greatest compliments ever paid to a Prime Minister by a parliamentarian — let alone a parliamentarian on the opposite side of the House. Admittedly, Powell has said subsequently of Britain's victory that 'The obstacles we overcame to retake the Falklands may have seemed large at the time. They are molehills compared with those which lie between us and the recovery of what this nation has lost in sovereignty during the last thirty years'; but, as we have already seen, he also felt that after the Falklands War 'nothing will be the same again'. By acting in the way she did, Thatcher proved to Powell's satisfaction that she had the determination to ignore world opinion and to take whatever steps were necessary to recover British territory from an enemy.

It is arguable whether Powell was right to attach such significance in his mind to this single incident — important as it was. Certainly, Thatcher has taken actions since — notably the Anglo-Irish Agreement — that have opened up a gulf between her and Powell larger and more impassable than ever before. More important, it is still questionable whether, when it comes to the EEC in particular, Thatcher and the rest of the Conservative party are acting from the same motives as Powell, even when they are perceived as nationalistic.

For example, the most likely explanation of Thatcher's conduct in her EEC negotiations still lies in her overriding concern that Britain should never again experience 'socialism' or, more accurately, an interventionist approach. The fact that she appears to acknowledge no conflict between her speech at Bruges and the 'guillotining' through Parliament of the Single European Act two years before either displays a total misunderstanding of what she has done, or an approach which has little in common with the passions displayed by Powell.

Despite the similarity of the vocabulary, there is often doubt whether the two have ever really spoken the same language. Her actions make more sense when seen as part of her general crusade against what she perceives as socialism on the continent. To the extent that the practical ramifications of sovereignty are impressed upon Thatcher by the realities of the single market, she may show frustration and annoyance. But this reaction cannot be equated with a genuine conversion on her part to parliamentary sovereignty in the sense that it is defined by Powell. If, for example, Thatcher approved of Delors' politics, it is unlikely whether she would still begrudge him his powers or be disinclined to work with him as a political ally. As a 'conviction politician', Thatcher is impatient with constitutional theories if they conflict with her political objectives.

The same could also be said of Lord Young, the British Cabinet Minister most closely associated with the run-up to 1992. He probably has no sympathy at all with high-Tory principles; he is one of the growing number of Tory politicians for whom action is more important than words, and who have nothing but impatience for those whose speeches have prepared the ground for their policies.

On 10 March 1989, he stated the view that 1992 was solely about extending free-enterprise policies across Europe; that 'pet projects' such as tax harmonization and worker directors would always be resisted by the British government.

Perhaps of greater significance, Commissioner Brittan, on the same day that Lord Young made these remarks, called for reductions in the figure of £65 billion that the EEC makes available in aid to industry. This is entirely consistent with Sir Leon's free-market approach; although it was in fact with Article 92 of the Treaty of Rome in mind that he spoke.

If Powell's Tory views were restricted exclusively to the economic field, he might find little exceptionable in the above positions, other than their naïveté and careless indifference to everything that is being said by other EEC governments. The point, however, is that, for Powell, they miss the entire point; even the word 'freedom', with which the Conservative party claims a privileged attachment, is not, in Powell's view, as straightforward as it sounds. A partial answer to what the Conservative party as a whole hopes to extract from Europe was proffered by Powell in a speech he made to some Young Conservatives in 1980:

> At the foot of the Young Conservatives' stationery appear the words 'The Key to a Free Future'. Unless I am mistaken, as an outside observer looking on, the Conservative party is in great danger of using the words 'free' and 'freedom' with insufficient analysis and definition of what it means by them. I say 'danger' advisedly: for words and the ideas for which they stand have a nasty habit of knocking on the back of the head politicians and parties

which use them thoughtlessly or rashly. So it is as a friendly spectator that I am going to ask the Conservative party some questions about its use of the word 'free'.

Who is to be free?

The expression 'free future' is obviously metonymical: it must be intended to mean that somebody or something will be 'free' in that future which the Conservative party and the Young Conservatives can influence. So my first question is: who or what will be 'free'? Be very careful how you answer, because the two possible answers have very different implications. One answer is: 'the nation will be free'; the other, 'the individual citizens (presumably all adult citizens) will be free'. I will take the first answer first, because it is the easier to handle, though none too easy, at that.

A 'free nation' can mean one or both of two things: a nation free externally, in the sense that all laws, policies, and acts of government generally which affect its citizens are made by its own institutions. In a nation 'free' in this sense, no laws will be made or taxes imposed or judgments judged by an external authority. In this sense, the Soviet Union, Zimbabwe and the United States are all 'free', but the United Kingdom is not, since its laws may now be made and defined, its taxes imposed, and its policies laid down by an external authority, namely the institutions of the EEC.

Now, the Conservative party officially approves of that status. In fact the Prime Minister, on alternate days, may be heard waxing enthusiastic about it. We must therefore conclude that a 'free future' in the sense of a nation externally 'free' is not the future to which Young Conservatives is the key. That is no small matter when you come to reflect upon it, since until recently that is what the people of this country did mean when they spoke or thought for example of 'fighting for freedom'. The charter in *Rule Britannia* that 'Britons never never shall be slaves' was not an allusion either to a free economy or to Lord Mansfield's celebrated judgment on slavery. It meant that Britain would always be a 'free nation' in the external sense.

Internal freedom

Thanks, as we have seen, to the Conservative party, *Rule Britannia* has turned out wrong: we have ceased to be a free nation in that sense. There is however another, internal sense, namely, a nation living under institutions which those using the adjective regard as affording or guaranteeing the freedom of individual citizens. Unlike external freedom, internal freedom is a matter of subjective judgment: we do not regard the Soviet Union as a free country in this sense; but neither (it appears) do the Russians regard the United Kingdom as a free country. Anyhow, we have now clearly moved on to the second possible answer to my original question – that in the Young Conservatives' 'free future' all adult citizens will be 'free'.

Freedom of action

I must now ask my second question: 'free to do what?' The word 'do' is perfectly satisfactory and sufficient in that context, because, although people talk also about 'free thought' and 'freedom of thought', they do not really mean it – they mean the free verbal or practical expression of thought, which is quite different and is covered by the question 'free to *do* what?' As nobody can know what I am thinking nor can I help thinking what I think, there is therefore no meaning in the category 'freedom' applied to thought as such. Believe me, there are as many 'free thinkers' in the Anglican Church as in the Society of Friends.

So, what is your answer? Not, surely, 'whatever he likes'? The freedom which you envisage is clearly not unlimited. By what, then, will it be limited? Surely, for one thing, by the law as duly made by the institutions of the EEC – your doing, not mine – or, in the absence of that, by our own subordinate Crown in Parliament? 'Yes, yes', you reply eagerly, 'but in our Young Conservative future fewer actions will be compelled or prohibited by law. That is what we mean by "freedom" and you are unreasonable to complain if the difference between being free or not free in our sense is only a question of degree.'

As a matter of fact, I wasn't going to make that point; I was going to take a different one and observe that you have defined the freedom of the individual by reference to the general opinion of contemporary society, as expressed by laws made or accepted. That is already a very profound modification of the notion of individual freedom; but it is not yet sufficient, because for this purpose the general opinion of a society extends beyond what is defined by law.

The closed shop

Your party has been agonizing over the closed shop and picketing. Why is it that your party has not found it possible to re-create the freedom of a man to employ or be employed without belonging to a trade union? That you have not done so is proved by the limitations of the so-called 'conscience clause'. I do assure you, it is not because Jim Prior and other members of the Cabinet are 'wet'. It is because of the opinion of society, derived from the belief, false in fact though it may be, that trade unions 'protect' the workers' wage and conditions. You cannot legislate a freedom which society will not uphold.

So wherever you look, you come back to society and general opinion. There was a time when it was an unquestioned freedom for a husband to beat his wife; but opinion changed, and there ceased to be such a freedom. There may equally come a time when areas of freedom, of individual unfettered decision, which we now collectively accept, will have ceased to be such, or vice versa. There is no repository, there are no tablets of stone, wherein are laid up those things which man, as man, is or ought to be free to do. The error of assuming so is the same error as underlies the whole business of 'human rights'. There is no escape out of the argument in a circle from a particular society to its members and back again.

Need for persuasion

The conclusion which I wish to leave with you is that, if the freedom to which Young Conservatives claim to hold the key is to withstand analysis, it must mean that they are themselves persuaded, and have set out to persuade others, that we should collectively behave differently: they wish, as it were, to change the nation's mind by exposing and expounding their own.

I have spent much of my political life commending to my fellow countrymen the advantages of allowing prices to settle themselves by means of markets, as compared with seeking to fix them by the rule of law. It is in my view misleading to describe the one process as more 'free' than the other, or as corresponding more with some preconceived notion of individual freedom. The market is a social process as much as – arguably more than – a statutory prices and incomes policy: the effect of an individual's free choice upon the one is about as great as upon the other.

The market commends itself to me, and I have sought to commend it to my fellow citizens, because it utilizes more effectively the mental and moral resources which are present in a society and minimizes the scope of individual human miscalculation.

If that is what you mean by a free economy, and if that is part at least of what you mean by a free society and a free future, I suggest to you that those terms need to be explored and analysed more thoroughly and explained more persuasively than I see the Conservative party doing at present.   (London, 4 October 1980)

It would be interesting to know how this speech was received by Powell's audience. Some may have thought that he was making rather too much of what, for them, is a relatively straightforward question. In one respect also, it is one of Powell's few speeches that betrays its age. Understandably, nobody then conducted the political debate on the assumption that Thatcher would be in office for over ten years. The country at that time still had vivid memories of state economic planning, state ownership, prices and incomes controls, high taxation, and legal immunities for trade unions. These issues were still on the political agenda. Had Thatcher been Prime Minister for only a single term – as was then the normal experience – the chances are that Labour would have reversed many of her reforms without too much difficulty on returning to power.

In these circumstances, most Conservatives knew what they meant by freedom, at least in the economic sphere. They wanted free enterprise; and for many, their faith in free enterprise had been nourished and enriched by the speeches of Powell in the 1960s and 1970s which often linked political and economic freedom with the freedom of the individual.

For many, the same considerations apply today. The fact that a democratic or a non-democratic state has the power to make its own laws does not, in their eyes, guarantee individual freedom if the policies which are pursued are authoritarian rather than libertarian in character. Powell's refusal to countenance this argument explains how he and some of his

former supporters drifted apart. It meant, too, that on the subject of the
EEC there was both a theoretical and practical difference between them.
Not only did Powell disagree that the EEC was on the side of free enterprise; he also considered the point to be the height of irrelevance. Powell
returned to the subject when he addressed a fringe meeting of Conservatives at their party conference in 1981:

> There are certain questions in politics about which there is no
> arguing. They are questions of such a nature that rational argu-
> ment cannot settle them. They belong to that side of man and of
> human society which lies beyond or beneath the domain of reason,
> and are themselves the starting point from which all reasoned
> argument and debate on ends and means proceed. For much of the
> time the answers to them are taken for granted, tacitly and even
> unconsciously; but from time to time they come to be the subject
> of dispute, in which members of the same society find themselves
> ranged on opposite sides.
>
> When that happens, one side or the other cannot be van-
> quished by force of argument: it can only be vanquished, in some
> form, by force itself. The questions about which I am speaking
> may therefore properly be called fighting questions.

'We' and 'they'

Supreme among these is freedom, not freedom in the individualistic sense of personal freedom, but freedom in the social sense of
common freedom, the freedom of 'us' from compulsion by 'them'.
Ask who are 'we' and who are 'they', and you will get only an
answer in a circle: 'we' are those at whose hands we accept compulsion, and 'they' are all those who are not 'we'. For convenience,
and with the imprecision always attendant upon inconvenience, let
us say that 'we' is the nation, and that the freedom in question is
(to use an outward-looking word) national independence or (to use
an inward-looking word) self-government.

Nations come into existence and nations cease to exist. They
can be destroyed by force. More often they perish when their
sense of identity – of being 'we' – dissolves. What happens to
them, and the fact that it has happened, is visible only after the
event; nor is there any magic formula or elixir which can be pre-

scribed or administered to maintain the existence of a nation. Its death or survival find expression, like a tragic denouement on the stage, through the conflict of actors who are themselves blind to the outcome and largely unconscious of the trends and forces which they are vocalizing.

Nationhood

No one can, by working from first principles, sustain or refute the imperative of nationhood: it is an imperative of instinct, of feeling, of passion, of prejudice even; and for that reason it is an imperative of force against force. That men will die for their nation and risk or sacrifice anything for its survival, is not fantasy, though the words in which it is described cannot be purged of metaphor: it is a fact about how men do behave in the observed world. For that reason freedom, pre-eminently and always, has been a fighting matter.

The question of the United Kingdom and its membership of the European Economic Community belongs in no lesser context than this. To remove it from this frame and seek to present it as a balance of economic calculation or of trading advantage is to degrade political discourse and insult the intelligence or the seriousness of the hearer.

Having described the terms in which he viewed the question, Powell asked of his Conservative audience what this meant for their party; and where they thought their party was heading.

A Conservative party which cannot present itself to the country as a national party suffers under a severe handicap; and the very arguments with which it might seek to exculpate itself are cruelly double-edged.

If membership of the EEC is defended by reference to alleged trading opportunities and the threat of even higher unemployment during the transition to a new trading pattern for Britain outside the Community, this is equivalent to asserting that freedom is a disposable asset to be exchanged for material advantage, and very debatable and temporary advantage at that — a remarkably embarrassing and unheroic stance to be caught commending to the British people.

A class party

If, on the other hand, the Conservative party invites the electorate to link national independence in its mind with Bennery and all things 'left' and to discern in membership of the Community a bulwark against the dangers of socialism, the implications are still more disreputable; for this is nothing other than saying that one would rather live under the tutelage of foreigners than incur the risk of one's fellow countrymen being free to make up their own minds. That would be to stamp the Conservative party as a class party with a vengeance, a slur the more damaging because there were in fact, at the time of the original debates, Conservatives inside and outside Parliament who did advocate membership on precisely that ground – blood brothers, no doubt, of those who in an earlier generation viewed the rise of Hitler with equanimity or approval as a safeguard against Communism.

Need for continued assent

So where is the Conservative party going to go? It is hopeless to put up the defence that, having signed the Treaty of Brussels and joined the Community, Britain is bound in honour – would that possibly be some ghost of *national* honour? – not to break its word but to take the consequences and 'make the best of it', as the saying goes.

Quite apart from the question whether any nation *can* effectively sign its liberty away – a proposition which we have ourselves historically been unwilling to admit in the case of others – there is the inconvenient fact that the right of Britain to withdraw from the Community was at all times plainly stated, and nowhere repudiated, both at accession and when, at the time of the 1975 referendum, the government officially informed the electorate and the world that if the answer were Yes, 'our continued membership will depend on the continued assent of Parliament'. In other words, our membership remained and remains revocable,

legally and morally, notwithstanding the referendum and notwithstanding any treaty or other commitment whatsoever.

Prospect of extrication

So, I repeat, where is the Conservative party going to? There are
none so dogged as those who know they have been wrong. There
are no words more disagreeable to eat than those which were first
pronounced reluctantly and under duress. Having overcome its
scruples and trampled on its instincts in 1972 as the price for keeping Heath and themselves in office, the Conservative party, by a
very human perversity, has proceeded to redouble and reiterate its
commitment to the Community like Ulysses lashing himself to the
mast. It might seem that the prospect of extrication was hopeless,
and the Conservative party was irrevocably bent on forcing the
electorate to choose between a Conservative government and the
recovery of its national selfhood.

I would not like to find myself left, or to leave you, with that
conclusion. Indeed, the very fact that some forty Conservative
Members of Parliament, however cautious the terminology of
their self-description (the Conservative European Reform Group),
have given this platform today to someone who once urged his
fellow electors to vote themselves back into national independence, is surely a portent of some encouragement.

A pragmatic party

But there is much more. If the general voice of the British public is
now declaring, as it is, ever more loudly and clearly its wish to
recall what was renounced on its behalf nine years ago, is there
anything to be ashamed of in a Parliamentary democracy if a political party moves to give effect to that wish? The Conservative
party has always seen itself as a pragmatic party as well as a
national party. In nothing has it been so pragmatic or, upon the
whole, so skilful as in catching the mind and purpose of the electorate and finding the means to give expression to them. The cynical
may say that as long as it can keep political power, the Conservative party will always go where it thinks the votes are; but

cynicism rarely matches reality. For myself, I would see little virtue
in a political party which deliberately set out to deny the nation
what it is calling for. If the people of this country wish again to be
a nation among nations, will the Conservative party not be their
spokesman?   (Blackpool, 14 October 1981)

This speech raises certain questions, some of which have been discussed
already. What, for example, is Powell's evidence for saying that the British
public preponderantly wishes *'to recall what was renounced on its behalf nine
years ago'*? Despite all Powell's arguments, it is still easy to gain the impression that, while many are unhappy about EEC membership, very few
equate Britain's loss of parliamentary sovereignty with defeat in war.

That is why some may wonder whether comparisons with 1938 are
relevant — particularly when those who will be voting for the first time at
the next general election have no memories at all of what Powell believes
constitutes a sovereign Parliament, let alone of the Second World War
itself. In any case, given that many of the people who voted 'yes' in the referendum did actually fight against Germany and oppose Munich, is it really
fair to compare their opposition to Bennery in 1975 with indifference to
Hitler prior to 1939? There *may* be a case for saying they were politically
naïve, but were they actually treacherous?

This, however, is a secondary issue. While many Conservatives do not
approach the EEC question on Powell's terms, they *are* beginning to
confront some of the practical questions of sovereignty that, Powell would
argue, arise from the very nature of the EEC. One question is as follows. If
these same Conservatives who are beginning to show unease about sovereignty were somehow convinced that there is no escape from political
union so long as Britain remains a full member of the EEC — that it is just a
matter of time, depending upon the willingness of countries like Britain to
accept or fight against it — would they accept this development as inevitable, or look in practical terms for a way out?

It is doubtful whether anyone can answer this question. The Conservative party would undoubtedly be very divided — and this is another
reason why every attempt would be made to duck the issue. It could be
argued that this is the purpose behind Margaret Thatcher's speech at
Bruges. It increases the temptation of believing that Britain can manage her
own affairs while remaining a full member of the Community. For those
who wish to arrest the momentum of political union, Thatcher is a doughty
champion. Even Nigel Lawson has said that neither the British government

nor the British Parliament is prepared to accept further Treaty amendments in this direction, and that 'those nations that are most vocal about their support for EMU now, tend to be those that are most assiduous in preserving barriers to free trade within the Community'. In other words, free trade can be achieved without the political ramifications. Provided the federalists are kept out of Downing Street, so the argument goes, 'federalism' can be checked.

(Powell rejects the use of the word 'federalism' in this context: as he explained to the editor, 'Federalism means the entrenched powers of the member states. This is a term which is commonly and erroneously used as a substitute for economic amalgamation. In any federal state, the powers of the component state are as inviolable as the powers conferred on the central authority.')

If this is the official position of the government, there is every incentive for Conservatives who want free trade and free enterprise to accept their leader's assurances. Those who will remain unhappy are those who fear that, yet again, Britain will be left behind and will be forced to accept the logical consequence of membership on much less advantageous terms than had political and monetary union been embraced enthusiastically from the start.

Thatcher will have none of this. True, she has said that Britain's 'destiny is in Europe, as part of the Community'; but mainly in the sense that 'The European Community is the *practical* [my italics] means by which Europe can ensure the future prosperity and security of its people in a world in which there are many other powerful nations and groups of nations.' In her speech, she makes clear that the EEC can never hope to be another United States of America; that 'to try to suppress nationhood and concentrate power at the centre of a European conglomerate would be highly damaging'; and that while Europe should seek on some issues 'to speak with a single voice', she says later that her idea of a united Europe is one 'which preserves the different traditions, parliamentary powers and sense of national pride in one's own country'.

Thus, the sentiments are clear enough. The details leave a little to be desired. Are the parliamentary powers she speaks of, for example, those in place before or after the Single European Act? Is it a question of thus far, and no further? If so, it can hardly satisfy those who share Powell's analysis.

Powell has said that 'The Prime Minister's instincts have a way of being right. By "right" I mean that they are in unison and sympathy with those of the great mass of the people' (London, April 1982). Actual examples sometimes help to bring the issues closer to home – for example, agriculture:

> Nineteen-eighty-four was the year of the great undeceiving. It was the year in which British farming awakened from its long dream. Gone were the heady days of 1972, when the Farmers' Unions not only of England, but of Wales, Scotland, and even Ulster, scenting untold prosperity and riches for their industry, threatened with fire and brimstone any wayward Member of Parliament who should dare to protest, let alone to vote, against the surrender of Britain's national right to make its own laws, impose its own taxes, judge its own judgments, and settle its own policies. 'Hold your noise about national independence and parliamentary sovereignty,' MPs were told; 'what do those baubles matter so long as agriculture is in the money?'
>
> How far off now those times appear! Who then looked forward to a day when the farmers' theme song would be conservation and when the brave new European organization would be organizing British dairy farmers out of business and preparing to do the same to the farmers of arable land carved out of former good cattle-rearing country? Where are those great agricultural bureaucrats hiding now, who got themselves cushy jobs wheeling and dealing in a far-away country called Europe?

These rhetorical questions paved the way for Powell's substantial point:

> 'What we have been witnessing is the emergence of the great incompatibilities, the incompatibility of British agriculture with continental agriculture, of the British economy with the continental economies, of the British parliamentary system with the constitutional dictatorship practised across the Channel, of British perspectives and purposes with those of Britain's continental neighbours – in short, of us with them.
>
> The conflict is only just starting. If you doubt it, watch and hear the European Parliament, that directly elected body which our national Parliament in a moment of madness rashly created in its own image to be a rod for our backs and a rallying point for our opponents. Do not imagine that the European Parliament is going to pipe down. I tell you it will pipe up and go on piping up until, in

covert league with the Commission, it has got the Council of Ministers under its thumb or alternately until the whole show has been smashed. All the chatter that proceeds from ministerial mouths is designed to cloak that reality. But the minds behind the mouths know the score and are already considering how to get out of the European scrape with no damage to themselves and possibly some benefit, if that can be arranged.

'*Until the whole show has been smashed*' is a revealing phrase. After nearly twenty years of full membership of the Community, it is unlikely that Britain could 'leave the Community' in the sense that it would have left after the 1975 referendum had the British people so decided. What is at stake now is whether Britain makes it impossible for the Community to evolve in the way that was always intended – to threaten, in short, to break up the whole 'show' – or at least to create a two-tier Europe in which Britain would figure prominently in the second, free-trade-area tier.

There are two distinct alternative approaches for Britain towards the Community. The one is to emphasize co-operation between sovereign member states and mutually advantageous arrangements compatible with the retention or recovery of full national independence, legislative and political. The other approach is to proceed towards merger by building upon that cession of national sovereignty which is implicit in the existing treaties. On 30 November last year [1984] the Prime Minister chose the occasion – of all possible occasions – afforded by the Franco-British conference at Avignon to utter a resounding rebuttal of the second and affirmation of the first of those approaches. For example, she declared, 'for nations of the European Community freely to work together and to strengthen their co-operation is just as worthy a purpose as a United States of Europe; to submerge their identity and variety would be contrary to the instincts of our peoples and therefore could not bear fruit.'

Thatcher also said on this occasion: 'We want to see greater unity of the Community market, greater unity of Community action in world affairs, greater unity of purpose and action in tackling unemployment and the other problems of our time, and greater unity in the development and application of new technology. That is what I understand by a united Europe.'

Where Thatcher was entirely on the same ground as Powell was in her statement, also in this speech, that 'I do not believe that we shall ever have a United States of Europe in the same way that there is a United States of America. The whole history of Europe is too different.' The same point was made at Bruges four years later.

Powell continued:

> A formulation more congenial to those who opposed and wish to see repealed the European Communities Act of 1972 could not be so plainly and yet so deftly framed. It is consistent, and I make no doubt it was intended to be consistent, with Britain resuming full political and parliamentary sovereignty untrammelled by such contraptions as the Common Agricultural Policy. But no Foreign Office official in the prime ministerial entourage could have found anything to insist upon having redrafted.
>
> (Dorchester, 2 January 1985)

And so the reader is finally brought to the significance of Thatcher's speech at Bruges. The jury is still out; but despite the enormous differences between Thatcher's and Powell's approach, he is perhaps entitled to draw some satisfaction from her words. But are both these politicians too late?

> Every door has to have a hinge on which it can turn. The same principle applies to politicians and political parties. Nineteen-eighty-eight was the year when the British public opened its eyes, yawned, looked around, and observed that it was about to be eaten alive by the European Economic Community. It did not like what it saw, and it prepared to be angry.

As the reader may remark himself, those sentiments have been expressed by Powell before; however, on this occasion Powell acknowledged the political problems this reversal could cause, even though:

> Fortunately, the political profession, to which, though compulsorily retired, I still belong, is equal to this most testing challenge. There is a solution. The solution is to go on using the same words while giving them the opposite meaning. Thus the two incompatible objectives of claiming total self-consistency and accomplishing a smart about-turn can be combined. Basically, it is the stratagem

of the man who got into a cinema without paying by walking backwards past the box office. An absolutely coruscating exhibition of artistry in this line of business is being exhibited at present. It would be a shame if the watching nation did not enjoy and appreciate it to the full; for the performance deserves your applause.

Everybody knows that the Prime Minister has always been a wholehearted and dedicated pro-European. She has said so over and over again, and she intends, quite consistently, to go on saying so over and over again – but the meaning is now the opposite.

Older than the Treaty of Rome

She was lately beside the lakeside in Italy, and what did she say? 'You do not need to doubt my commitment to Europe.' No, of course not, Prime Minister; but what did she add? '*A Europe which is older than the Treaty of Rome*'. One does not need to be an over-subtle logician to observe that 'a Europe older than the Treaty of Rome', the treaty which set the EEC up, must be a Europe without the EEC. The artistry is superb. It was prepared in a little-noted but important passage in her celebrated speech at Bruges. There, in the text distributed if not drafted for her by the Foreign Office, she declared that 'the European Community is one manifestation of the European identity; *but it is not the only one*. We' – the British, that must mean – 'shall always look on Warsaw, Prague, and Budapest as great European cities.' Yes; and they have another thing in common too – they are none of them in the EEC.

So the Prime Minister, who speaks of course for Her Majesty's government and for the Conservative party, is still unalterably 'committed to Europe'. Who dare charge her or them with inconsistency? But all along, apparently when they said 'Europe' they didn't mean the EEC at all. So they can justifiably – dare I say? – 'rejoice, rejoice' in their unswerving commitment, which no longer need include the Treaty of Rome – or presumably the Treaty of Brussels.

A tightrope performance

It was, however, in order obligatorily to comply with those Treaties, as extended by the European Single Act of 1985, that

Conservative majorities in Parliament solemnly repudiated and abjured the legislative and fiscal supremacy of Parliament itself. But has not Mrs Thatcher declared at Bruges that 'the best way to build a successful European community is "co-operation between independent sovereign states ... a way which preserves the parliamentary powers of one's own country"?'

The audacity and brilliance of the operation is almost breathtaking. Indeed, like those watching a tightrope performance of high professional skill, one is scared to cheer, lest premature applause might upset the act. There was a famous passage in British political history when it was made a charge against Disraeli that he had caught the Whigs bathing and stolen their clothes. No such charge can be made against the present Prime Minister. Admittedly, what she is saying now is substantially what the Labour party had been saying all the time since Gaitskell; but steal their clothes she did not. What happened was different. In an eruption of nudist enthusiasm, the Labour party divested themselves of every stitch of raiment, did the stuff all up in a neat parcel, and popped round and left it on the doorstep of No. 10. I defy anybody to call that stealing.

The beauty of all this is that nobody need suffer embarrassment. Nobody, politician or publicist, need fear to be force-fed with the words that he had been innocently using all down the years in order to remain respectable and in the fashion. It just turns out that all the time he really meant something different. Pride, sincerity, honesty, and all those other virtues for which we admire our politicians will remain intact. The British people, however, who woke up just in the nick of time, are going to get their way. They are not going to be eaten alive after all. What else did the Prime Minister mean in her recent interview in *The Times*: 'People who wanted a federal Europe are very cross. Everybody else is cheering like mad'? (London, 2 November 1988)

CHAPTER NINE

NATION STATE

Never again, by the necessity of an axiom, will an Englishman live for his country or die for his country: the country for which people live and die was obsolete, and we have abolished it

ENOCH POWELL

The speeches in this book were made over a period of some fifteen years. Never during this period did Powell's opposition to the EEC falter. He considered it always to be the supreme issue facing the nation. As we have seen, Powell even entertained serious doubts as to whether he was right to remain a Member of Parliament once the European Communities Act of 1972 received the Royal Assent.

One reason for his deciding to seek re-election was because he cared as much about Ulster as he did about withdrawing from the EEC; and it should not be forgotten that between October 1974 and his 'compulsory retirement' from Parliament in June 1987, Powell was a loyal member of the Official Unionist Party and answerable in the first instance to his Northern Ireland constituents in South Down. This, however, gave rise to no conflict of loyalty; Powell's concern for the sovereignty of Parliament was matched by his determination to help maintain Ulster within the United Kingdom. Indeed, he saw the two issues as connected, and cited them both as examples of Britain's growing indifference to the responsibilities and privileges of nationhood.

Thus, although this book is exclusively concerned with the European Community and 1992, the speeches reproduced often reveal the anger and frustration aroused in Powell by events surrounding Ulster and, in particular, by the Anglo-Irish Agreement, which was signed on 15 November 1985.

Nowhere is the Ulster dimension more important than in Powell's views on defence and his strictures upon the foreign and defence policies of the United States. He suspected that the British Foreign Office, under pressure from the United States, was prepared to sacrifice Ulster in order to uphold the strength and objectives of NATO; he believed that NATO's defence strategy rested upon a fallacy; but even had he thought otherwise, Powell would still have criticized what he regarded as the duplicity of British governments in asserting the indissolubility of Ulster's union with the United Kingdom, while doing, as he argued, all in their power to undermine it.

There are some Conservatives who agree with Powell that the government's policy towards Northern Ireland is both mistaken and dangerous; but there are not many who subscribe to his analysis of the American factor, or share his belief that United States and United Kingdom interests are antagonistic to one another. On the contrary, those of them who are also opposed to Britain's EEC membership tend to regard the 'special relationship' between the United States and Britain as being of much greater value than Britain's links with the EEC; they would point to the support – some would say, decisive support – given by America to Britain at the time of the Falklands War as further testimony to this fact; and although geographically Britain is part of Europe, for many opponents of the EEC – the 'Atlanticists' – this country's relationship with the United States is the aspect of foreign policy that must be safeguarded at all costs.

As we have seen, this is *not* Powell's view. Emotionally and intellectually, he would consider himself a 'European', if he thought such a being was capable of classification and definition. His suspicions of the United States have led him to question whether any credence can be placed upon public pronouncements emanating from the British government in defence or foreign-policy matters. With his classical training, he has analysed in the smallest detail the phraseology of ministerial statements upon Ulster and defence, and has detected within them support for what he believes to be United States strategic designs.

All this is relevant to Powell's objections to Britain's membership of the EEC, in so far as he regards it as yet another example of Britain's failure to act independently and in her own interests. His analysis of the Ulster problem has led him to distrust in the most absolute terms everything to do with the United States and indeed with the British political Establishment, of which he had once been an awkward – but, nevertheless, an acknowledged – member. He believes that both Britain's membership of the

EEC and its alleged willingness to discard Northern Ireland are motivated by the desire to maintain the special relationship with the United States.

Powell considers this stance to be cowardly, and demeaning for a self-respecting nation. But, as he told a Conservative audience at their party conference in 1987, 'there are apparently some who believe that the British nation itself has become obsolete or, at least, that the British have ceased to care about the political independence that was renounced on their behalf.' Thus, in the final analysis, the extent to which the reader sympathizes with Powell's analysis will depend upon whether or not he shares Powell's concept of nationhood and political independence. Some feel that the nation state is obsolete, not because they have ceased to care about their country, but because they have concluded that global political and economic realities negate the traditional methods of safeguarding their independence.

Powell may not admit this possibility openly in his EEC speeches; indeed, he would contest the point. But he has also expressed his conviction that 'at the end of a lifetime in politics, when a man looks back, he discovers that the things he has most opposed have come to pass and that nearly all the objects he set out with are not merely not accomplished, but seem to belong to a different world from the one he lives in.'

Does nationhood fall into this category? Nobody can escape the impression, after reading Powell's speeches, that the continuance or not of the nation state is the question that Powell is in effect addressing. Each individual must, therefore, ask himself whether he considers this question to be anachronistic or as fundamental as it has ever been? In attempting to supply Powell's answer, both in this chapter and in the next, a number of points need to be reiterated.

The first is to remember, particularly bearing 1992 in mind, that Powell is not opposed to close trading links with Europe. This is where his analysis of the implications of a single European market is of great topical interest. A key issue is whether businessmen in the Community ought to be preparing for free trade in Europe or for economic and political integration. In welcoming the building of a Channel tunnel – rather to the surprise of some of his supporters – Powell placed both the free trade and the 1992 aspects of the EEC debate in their proper context.

In those far-off days – and how far-off they seem! – when Mr Heath's government swerved into policies which many of us found unrecognizable and unacceptable, I was amongst those opposed to the project of a Channel tunnel. Recent events have stirred those memories and prompted me to recur to the subject.

There are two separate issues. One is whether there ought to be a fixed cross-Channel link. The other is who ought to pay for it. I have decided views on both. Taking the second first, not a penny of public money ought to be put behind it. This is just the sort of proposal which makes all the wrong bells ring: once public money comes in through the door, political caution and good judgment go out of the window. Only if private capital will genuinely risk financing the operation dare I believe that the probable odds are in favour and that all the relevant economic aspects bearing upon success have been critically weighed. Even so, promoters can get it wrong; but there will be no new albatross hung around the tax-payers' necks.

Powell then proceeded to the desirability of the tunnel itself:

The British public favours me from day to day with an extensive correspondence; and I have been struck by how many of those who write to me assume I would be hostile to this project, partly because they know of my dedicated and continuing hostility to Britain's membership of the European Economic Community, and partly also because I have never concealed my conviction that the geographical insularity of Great Britain is still of decisive impor-tance for this nation's military defence. My correspondents' as-sumption is in fact mistaken on both counts. If genuine private capital will genuinely finance a Channel fixed link, I say hoorah! and the best of luck to it, and will cheerfully vote for any enabling legislation that may be requisite if it can pass the scrutiny of a select committee.

Defence implications

A Channel bridge and tunnel are utterly irrelevant to Britain's defence. Had they existed in June 1940, we would surely have smashed them so effectively that the Luftwaffe would still have had to dash itself to pieces in the vain attempt to cover a seaborne invasion. I assume of course that it will be made a condition of construction that any facilities necessary for destruction – though not, presumably, primed! – are built into the design and fabric from the outset.

There remains admittedly a more subtle risk to be considered, namely, that ease of transit might tempt Britain at some time in the future to throw its last reserves into a continental battle of which the outcome would not determine its own survival. As to this, I can only observe that the decision not to commit our fighters in 1940 to the lost Battle of France was taken, and rightly taken, despite the facility with which that transfer could have been made. I disregard, because it belongs to a much larger context, the possibility that increased facility of communication with the continent could result in still larger American reserves being held in these islands and thus in raising the present level of America's power to influence the strategic stance of the United Kingdom.

The economics

Turning secondly from defence to economics, I endorse unreservedly anything which improves the facility of exchange of goods and services between the inhabitants of the United Kingdom and the outside world, near or far. I confess to a free trader's conviction that freedom and ease of trade must tend to the increase of mutual well-being.

This has nothing to do with the EEC. The Common Market is not about free trade. So far as it is about economic ends at all, it is about the regulation and restraint of trade. Nothing that improves the communications of Britain with the continent carries any implication that there should be a common authority exercising legislative, judicial, and policy-making powers over the populations of the component states.

One of the beauties of free trade is that it is a-political: you do not have to browbeat or overrule anybody else in order to enjoy its blessings for yourself. It is a game at which, like Patience, one can play; and like common sense it can be practised with impunity and advantage in the midst of a crazy world. Since gold was eliminated as a monetary medium and replaced by paper and credit, there has been no need to enter into mutual agreements with other countries that they will open their markets to the outside world or indeed conduct their own affairs in one way rather than another. If

Richard Cobden had lived, as we have the good fortune to live, in a world of freely floating paper currencies, he would never have bothered to negotiate a trade treaty with France nor had to go to the trouble of explaining elementary economics to the Emperor Napoleon III or the Empress Eugenie.

The exchange rate

Let the rest of the world beat its path to our door, whether with mousetraps or computers, while practising the stupidest protectionism in their own countries, the exchange rate will automatically ensure that they have either to purchase from us or to invest with us in return whatever seems to them the equivalent value in goods and services. I am all for them getting our goods and services, and for us getting theirs, at the lowest transport cost possible. It is common sense not to pay more for anything than one has to – no point in going by stage coach if you can travel by train.

Three cheers then for the Channel link, provided the investment in it is profitable – provided, that is to say, that its cost is more than offset by the advantage which is likely to accrue for transportation and communication. The likelihood is not a question I would entrust to any judgment but that of the market. If promoters come forward to Parliament and say 'Here is the scheme, we will put our own capital behind it', then I for one am disposed to give them my parliamentary blessing and wish them the best of luck from an anti-Common Market nationalist.

(Reading, 4 November 1985)

Nobody who endorses 'unreservedly anything which improves the facility of exchange of goods and services between the inhabitants of the United Kingdom and the outside world, near or far' can be fairly accused of economic insularity. To the extent that 1992 promotes this 'facility' between the United Kingdom and the rest of the EEC, Powell would applaud it. But, as we have seen, Powell's view is that 'The Common Market is not about free trade'; it is about politics.

Economics are politics in disguise. The embarrassing inability of the [Conservative] Opposition to resolve, or even openly to recognize and debate, its internal differences over economic policy is not due to the Leader and her colleagues having studied different textbooks or sat at the feet of different professors of economics.

Matters of exchange rates, balance of payments, monetary systems, trading practices, are not resolved by economic theories: they are expressions of political will and cannot be handled consistently or intelligibly to the public nor (still less) inspiringly, unless the individual decisions and policies can be consciously related to a political philosophy and view of the world. To decide what to do or not to do about sterling, you must first know whether Britain is a nation and what a nation is; you must know of what sort of political purpose these economic phenomena are to be the manifestations and instruments.

(Liverpool, 17 November 1978)

'You must first know whether Britain is a nation and what a nation is': for Powell, even a technical discussion of 1992 or the wider economic ramifications of integrating the British economy with those of her continental partners keeps coming back to the same question. So is the nation State obsolete, or not?

The classic statement in the whole [referendum] campaign was that of Edward Heath in the Oxford Union debate. He asserted, as he has many times done before, that the nation State is obsolete in the modern world and that this is the justification, not to say necessity, for the United Kingdom being part of the EEC.

Few seem to have recognized how far-reaching is the significance of that assertion. I believe it to be unfounded both as regards the past and the future; but it defines the central battleground of the struggle for and against British membership, of which the referendum marked the end of one phase and the opening of the next.

The nation State

The term 'nation State' demands close attention. Mr Heath does not mean that *the State* is obsolete – the EEC itself is to be in all respects a State, with all the powers, internal and external, characteristic of a State: nations may continue in other contexts – ethnic, sentimental, cultural, and so on – but as States, as political entities recognizing no superior authority, they are obsolete.

The nation State has much older and deeper roots than Mr Heath seems to be aware. I do not know if the doctrine that the nation State arose in the 19th century was still being taught at Oxford in the 1930s: but it is erroneous. The nation State reaches back far into the origins of Europe itself and perhaps beyond. If Europe was not always a Europe of nations, it was always a Europe in which nations existed, and were taken for granted, as a basic form of the State.

Declaration of Arbroath

In 1320 the barons of Scotland wrote to the Pope, whose approval was being solicited by their English aggressors, a letter which has come to be known as the Declaration of Arbroath. They told the Pope that 'the Scots, one of many famous nations, took possession of their home in the West and have held it free of all bondage ever since', and that 'as long as but a hundred of us remain alive, never will we under any circumstances be brought under English rule. It is in truth not for glory nor riches nor honour that we are fighting but for freedom. The King of the English ought to be satisfied with what belongs to him and leave us Scots in peace, who live in this poor little Scotland, beyond which there is no dwelling place at all, and covet nothing but our own.'

This is the authentic and valid description of the nation State: a homogeneous people – at least a people believing themselves homogeneous – who possess a naturally defined territory and acknowledge no superior authority – or at any rate no superior *secular* authority, a limitation that the English and the Scots both rejected at the Reformation.

The new State

If the nation State is now obsolete, and in particular if the United Kingdom has ceased to be a nation State and become part of a larger, non-nation State, two consequences of immense and little-considered purport follow. First, the new West European State is by definition not homogeneous, because otherwise it too would be a nation State and therefore obsolete. Secondly, the new State consists, politically speaking, not of nations (which have been superseded) but of individuals.

Of such a State one thing can be asserted with absolute certainty: it cannot, in any sense that we recognize, be democratic and must therefore be authoritarian; for democracy implies the acceptance of majority decision, and this in turn presupposes homogeneity – in the sense that the minorities identify themselves with the whole sufficiently to place the interests of the whole above their own.

Whenever this identification is absent or ceases, as for example when the Irish Nationalists arrived in the Victorian Parliament, representative democratic government becomes impossible and either it is superseded by coercion or the State itself must be broken up. The idea that a mass of humanity is turned into a democracy by giving it an assembly directly elected by universal suffrage is a delusion which the West has expiated by now with with a good deal of other people's blood.

Something else can be asserted with equal assurance about the new non-nation State. Being composed of individuals, and neither being a society itself nor comprising any societies other than private societies, it must be materialistic and individualistic. The Mediterranean world under the Roman emperors gives us some picture of a civilization from which nation States have been eliminated. I wonder if those who use the current terms of commendation for British membership of the EEC understand that this is what they are describing.

Powell then proceeded to challenge the fundamental reason normally advanced for integrating Britain into a new, European, political unit.

'Britain will be more prosperous in the EEC.' 'The British will have more power and influence in the world in the Community.' 'Britain has the opportunity to lead Europe.' These are trick sentences. The words 'Britain' and 'the British' are used as if they meant the British nation and are intended so to be understood: but the statements in which they stand, though they appear to be political statements, presuppose the non-existence of the British nation, the prior elimination of the British nation State.

'The British' in statements such as these is merely the plural of 'a Briton'. 'Britain' and 'the British' denote simply those of the Community's inhabitants who live in Britain, speak English, eat fish and chips, and exhibit other non-political symptoms associated with the people of this island. Britons *as individuals* will have higher incomes, and some of them *as individuals* will occupy prominent positions in a more powerful State.

Never again, by the necessity of an axiom, will an Englishman live for his country or die for his country: the country for which people live and die was obsolete, and we have abolished it.

Or not quite yet. No, not yet. The referendum is not a verdict, after which the prisoner is hanged forthwith. It is no more than provisional, as all electoral decisions are provisional. It is as little final as the outcome of a general election can commit us irrevocably to Mr Heath's form of socialism, or to Mr Benn's form of capitalism. This will be so, as long as one Parliament can alter or undo whatever that or any other Parliament has done. Hence those golden words in the government's referendum pamphlet: 'Our continued membership will depend on the continuing assent of Parliament.'   (*Daily Telegraph*, 9 June 1975)

Powell's mention of Tony Benn offers the excuse to quote Benn himself speaking upon exactly the same point in the House of Commons. The similarity of their approach is striking: but unlike Powell, Benn continues to enjoy the privilege, as a Member of Parliament, to bring issues immediately to the attention of the House of Commons:

It would be inconceivable for the House to adjourn for Easter without recording the fact that last Friday [13 March 1989] the High Court disallowed an Act which was passed by this House and the House of Lords and received Royal Assent – the Merchant Shipping Act 1988. The High Court referred the case to the European Court.... I want to make it clear to the House that we are absolutely impotent unless we repeal Section 2 of the European Communities Act. It is no good talking about being a good European. We are all good Europeans; that is a matter of geography and not a matter of sentiment. Are the arrangements under which we are governed such that we have broken the link between the electorate and the laws under which they are governed? I am an old parliamentary hand – perhaps I have been here too long – but I was brought up to believe, and I still believe, that when people vote in an election they must be entitled to know that the party for which they vote, if it has a majority, will be able to enact laws under which they will be governed. That is no longer true. Any party elected, whether it is the Conservative party or the Labour party can no longer say to the electorate, 'Vote for me and if I have a majority I shall pass that law', because if that law is contrary to Common Market law, British judges will apply Community law.

(*Hansard*, 13 March 1989 c. 56–8)

In fact, the Court of Appeal ruled that the High Court had been mistaken in blocking the application of the 1988 Merchant Shipping Act although, at the time of writing, the matter may still go for appeal to the House of Lords.

Powell's mention of the Reformation sheds further light upon his understanding of nationhood, and particularly English nationhood. He regards the Church of England as an integral part of the English nation. He also believes the Church of England to be part of the Catholic – although not the *Roman* Catholic – Church. Readers are referred to Cardinal Newman's *Apologia pro vita sua* (1864) for the definitive answer to this particular point. It is beyond the scope of this book.

On the other hand, no description of Powell's views on nationhood would be complete without reference to his membership of the Church of England; and it is particularly pertinent to the EEC debate to consider why the visit to the United Kingdom of His Holiness Pope John Paul II in 1982 was a source of such concern to Powell. In expressing his objections towards the Pope making an official visit – a visit that eventually took place two years after Powell publicly raised the issue and, incidentally, at the time of the Falklands War – Powell provides further material for understanding his opposition to Britain's EEC membership. Having made clear at the outset that the issue of the Pope's visit was neither 'religious', 'credal', 'theological', 'liturgical', nor 'ecclesiastical', but '*political*', Powell went on to discuss the implications:

It is a peculiarity of this political issue that it affects differently different parts of the State. Directly, it involves Northern Ireland and Wales not at all. Since the disestablishment of the Church in Ireland in 1869 and in Wales in 1914 no single proposition regarding the relationship of Church and State any longer holds good for the United Kingdom as a whole. The political implications of a papal visit only concern Wales and Ulster indirectly, by virtue of their being integral parts of the same United Kingdom as Scotland and England. In Scotland and in England, on the other hand, which do comprise over ninety per cent of the population of the whole kingdom, there is an established national Church, of which the sovereign is either (as in England) the governor or (as in Scotland) shares the headship.

Secular and religious

There is, so far as I am aware, no parallel to this anywhere in the world. Many states regulate and even subsidize the practice of religion; others are explicitly secular, some of them proclaiming aggressively the total separation of Church and State; others express themselves as approving and supporting a particular religion, sect, or church; in yet others again the sovereigns are themselves gods or incarnations of gods. In England and Scotland alone, under the only true – that is, prescriptive – monarchy in the world, does the person of the monarch unite the headship of the State and the headship of the Church: the Church is both secular and religious, and this remains true despite the fact that religious dissent and diversity enjoy complete toleration and freedom within our country.

Nevertheless the relationship of the Crown to the Church of Scotland and its supreme body, the General Assembly, is profoundly different from its relationship to the Church of England, and the significance of that relationship is immensely greater in England than in Scotland – so much so, that the question of a papal visit could be said to be, in the first place, an essentially English question. Only in England is the source of lawful authority in the national Church identical with the source of secular authority in the United Kingdom, namely, the Crown in Parliament, by which, or by the consent of which, the worship and doctrine of the Church of England continue to be determined. Only in England is the Crown the supreme judicial authority in the national Church. Thus the political nerve which is directly touched by a papal visit is an English nerve, though the consequences are transmitted through the whole body politic because it is the sovereignty and independence of the nation as a whole which they ultimately affect.

Queen and Pope

It is constitutionally and logically unthinkable for England to contain both the Queen and the Pope. Before that could happen, the essential character of the one or the other would have had to be surrendered. If the Queen is 'on Earth supreme governor of the Church in England', then His Holiness is not in this realm 'Christ's vicar upon Earth'. Either the Pope's authority is not universal or the Church of England is not the Catholic and Apostolic Church in this land.

The assertion which His Holiness personifies and the assertion which Her Majesty personifies are irreconcilable. Like so many others, this irresolvable conflict can be endured at a respectful distance. Even in entering the Vatican, the Queen leaves the conflict undisturbed, since the claim which her existence asserts is a claim to national and not to universal supremacy. Let no one suppose, however, that when a Pope sets foot on the soil of England, one claim, one assertion, has not by that very act given place to the other.

It is not difficult to know which it would be. Not one jot of its claim will – or indeed can, without forfeiting its nature – the papacy abate. The bull *Regnans in Excelsis*, which absolved the subjects of the first Elizabeth from their allegiance to a heretical monarch, will remain unrecalled. The bull *Apostolicae Curae* will continue to declare that the priests of the Church of England are no priests and its sacraments are no sacraments. I make no complaint of all this; those who expect the Roman Church to renounce its imperial heritage deceive themselves. My complaint lies in the other direction. It lies against those who are ready on every occasion to renounce their national inheritance of liberty and sovereignty.

Royal supremacy

The royal supremacy in the Church of England is no mere fiction and historical relic that has survived from the Tudor age. It is a living reality, without which the Church of England could not *be* the Church of England and the British nation could not *be* the British nation. In England the supremacy of the Crown in Parliament is the guarantee to millions that their inheritance in the Church can never be taken away from them by arbitrary decision or clerical fashion and that the Church of England will never be narrowed into one sect among other sects nor dissolved and lost in an international and amorphous Christianity. But the British nation as a whole, of which England and the English are but a part, nevertheless shares in that national consciousness of independent identity of which the royal supremacy is not the least potent expression.

Eight years ago the Crown in Parliament found it possible solemnly to renounce the sole right not only to tax the Queen's subjects but to make the laws of this realm and to judge its causes.

The sovereign, though still declared 'supreme as well in all spiritual and ecclesiastical things or causes as temporal', is now almost daily dragged, by her own subjects amongst others, before foreign courts, to be censured and her judgments overturned. It may perhaps be thought an exercise in pedantry and historicism to discuss the implications of a papal visit to Great Britain when apparently more real aspects of national sovereignty – aspects, too, unambiguously applicable to the whole United Kingdom – have been lost and the campaign to regain them has scarcely begun. I do not agree. The full realization of our nationhood was achieved in the Reformation, and its English manifestation was the substitution of the royal supremacy for the Roman *imperium*. Symbols live when concrete things perish. The last possessions of a nation, without which it cannot renew itself, are its national symbols. Can the British people in 1980 really be indifferent when their government is able to sacrifice those symbols without even appearing to be conscious that it is doing so?   (East Grinstead, 5 December 1980)

The points that Powell makes in this speech are also fundamental to the EEC debate. In a different context, he is repeating sentiments he has expressed before – for example, 'my complaint lies against those who are ready on *every* occasion to renounce their national inheritance of liberty and sovereignty.' Of special interest is his assertion that the royal supremacy *in the Church of England* is one of the essential factors in constituting the British nation; this means that any attempt to disestablish the Church, or to remove Parliament's right to have the final say on *all* matters – including doctrinal – relating to the Church of England is, in Powell's opinion, tantamount to an assault upon the nation itself. The issue strikes the very same nerve that has been assaulted by Britain's membership of the European Community.

The speech reveals something else. Powell's concern is for the *United Kingdom*; but at a time when nationalism in Scotland and Wales is again in the ascendant, it is salutary to be reminded of how, for some, *England* still occupies a special place in the British nation. The implications, perhaps, are that there are lengths to which England cannot go, even if it means risking the unity of the United Kingdom, let alone Europe.

In October 1805 His Britannic Majesty George III was at war with the Emperor of the French, Napoleon Bonaparte. As his navy sailed into battle against the combined fleets of France and Spain, the admiral ordered the signal 'Nelson confides that every man this day will do his duty'. The signal officer suggested that, as he would have to spell out letter by letter both 'Nelson' and 'confides', there would not be time to complete the signal before the engagement began. Could he substitute 'England expects', which could be signalled with two flags only? Nelson assented, and so the message went out to the fleet at Trafalgar and to succeeding generations.

'England'. The nation at war with France and Spain was the United Kingdom of Great Britain and Ireland – a description at that time only four years old. In 1707 the Scottish Parliament had been merged with the English Parliament. In 1800 the Irish Parliament had been merged with the Parliament of Great Britain. These were events which the political genius of the English had made possible and inevitable. All government and all society rest upon consent, and the English have never been governed otherwise than with their consent. What they had created was a unique device for combining the unlimited authority vested in an ancient hereditary monarchy with the unfettered self-expression of a proud though dutiful people.

English qualities

The qualities with which the logically insoluble problem was solved were English qualities: tolerance and forbearance, respect for history, for forms and precedents, and not least (be it added) a facility for mutually understood and conventionally approved make-believe. For those qualities in action there is a single word: debate, debate in the sense specific to that Parliament which the same English qualities converted from a feudal institution of the kind common to all Western Europe into the unique instrument of national self-expression. It matched the natural propensity of those who, as they told Henry Bolingbroke, 'bin commen out of all England' to find consent through tolerant and structured discourse.

In that English Parliament, and in the House which George II, still more German than English, was one day to call 'that damned House of Commons', the Welsh had already found a place and voice when the Scots made the deliberate decision, which they have never yet revoked, to be one parliamentary nation with the rest of Great Britain. The unique instrument the English had forged proved equal to the enterprise. It was repeated afterwards with the third kingdom in the British Isles; and who knows whether, if the indispensable ingredient of mutual tolerance had not been omitted, that enterprise too would not have succeeded? Even so, the equality of citizen rights inseparable from the institution of Parliament remains the only talisman by which today the people of the United Kingdom's outlying province can be 'godly and quietly governed'.

A parliamentary nation

The England which expects its people to do their duty in the hour of peril is a parliamentary nation. The soul of that liberty with which its citizens associate their nationhood is the right to live under laws which are made by that Parliament and government which is consented to by that Parliament.

It is a quarter of a century since I last had the honour to propose this toast to this Royal Society [The Royal Society of St George, at a banquet at Guildhall]. At that time the nation was in the middle of the pangs of withdrawal from empire. To a generation born and brought up in the heady atmosphere of empire and accustomed to equate the greatness of England with the extent of territory coloured red on the globe and the unimaginable millions of human beings who were subjects of the Crown, it was hard, though necessary, to recognize that England's real greatness had never ceased to lie here in our own islands and our own folk and to re-learn the old imperial saying in a new but juster form, 'What do they know of England who aught but England know?'

A greater peril

Today, twenty-five years after, when only a few microscopic specks of red are still scattered across the oceans and the imperial dream – for dream it always was – has dissolved into the conventional delusion of Commonwealth, the English stand in a different but a greater peril. The trauma of lost empire has been succeeded by the disease of self-depreciation. It has become the prevalent, not to say official, assumption that we the English can no longer live under the institutions which England created: the pride and boast of the Englishman that he lives under no laws but those he has made himself and obeys no government but that which he has chosen have become subjects for pity or ridicule. The nation is too small, we are told, too unimportant, too contemptible to be any longer what the Englishman once meant by being free.

A sub-species

Our Parliament has formally and comprehensively renounced its old exclusive right to make law and to assent to taxation. We are only a sub-species now of the genus European. We live under a European court, a European council, and a European Parliament (so it calls itself); their rules override our laws, their verdicts override our courts, their legislature dictates to our Parliament.

The rights of a freeborn Englishman, which used to be secured to him by his native institutions, are no longer good enough. On pain of displeasing an outside world that lived under horrid tyrannies long after England was self-governing, we petition foreign judges sitting on the continent to declare and enforce our rights by interpreting at their discretion a document which no English lawyer – I almost said no writer of decent English – would imagine in a nightmare. We tolerate these judges telling the House of Commons what the House of Commons shall or shall not do.

Bitterest of all, and freshest in our minds today, the English, who once were wont, if allies failed, to defend themselves alone against 'the three corners of the world in arms', accept with apparent docility the occupation of their soil in time of peace by self-appointed protectors, as though the Roman legions were still stationed at York and Caerleon, and we pay them the humiliating tribute of conforming ourselves to their policies, their strategies, and their philosophy.

England has forgotten itself. In the distorting mirror which the outside world is happy enough to hold up to us, we behold, where previously we discerned the bullfrog monster of a world-wide empire, the suppliant figure of an insignificant dwarf.

The latter image is as false and foolish as the former. Nothing has so altered in reality that the resources and native capabilities of England are no longer equal to define and to achieve aims no less our own and no less noble than those who went before us defined and achieved. The Queen Elizabeth who this week in the thirty-fifth year of her reign attained her sixtieth year may say with as good a right as did the first of her royal name in the England and the world of four centuries ago:

> 'That great supremacy
> Where we do reign we will alone uphold
> Withough the assistance of a mortal hand.'

(London, 22 April 1986)

CHAPTER TEN

REVERTING TO TYPE?

It was always a generation which did not remember – or it was very often a generation which did not remember – those who had defended and developed the characteristic constitutional rights of the United Kingdom in the past, who have done the same in their own time.

ENOCH POWELL

Most of the questions that anyone might wish to ask of Powell about the European Community are answered in his own speeches. This is true of all the political subjects to which he has given his attention throughout his political career. The key to understanding Powell is through his own words. 'Understanding' is of course not the same as 'agreement': but many of the criticisms directed at Powell in the past have been born not of disagreement, but of a careless reading of what he has said. Powell demands a level of attention from his audience that is often lacking in his critics.

The European Community, however, raises issues of exceptional gravity and sensitivity. Powell has even cast doubt upon whether they can be resolved by debate or discussion at all – or at least, whether the central question of British nationhood, to which all the others are secondary, can be disposed of by argument. As he once explained, in a speech in May 1978:

> The answer to the real question is wholly subjective, and cannot be arrived at by a process of reasoning from facts – not even

agreed facts. It is in short, a matter of prejudice. A man who says 'I feel myself to be an Englishman' and another who says 'I feel myself to be a European' cannot argue their difference out by reasoning, no more than a man who says 'my supreme loyalty under God is to the Queen' and another who says 'my supreme loyalty is to the Treaty of Rome and to the European Court as its interpreter.' They can fight about their difference, but they cannot settle it by reason.

Powell provides more than enough material in his speeches for the reader to judge the issues in so far as it is possible to do so. But judging the issues is not the same as determining the fundamental question. And at the end of the day, the individual must ask himself what kind of country he wishes to live in.

That said, it is fitting that this short volume of Powell's speeches should conclude with Powell himself being allowed the final say. An interview seemed to be the best way of bringing this analysis to as topical a conclusion as possible, and of emphasizing again the most salient points in Powell's argument. Our conversation went as follows.

How seriously do you regard 1992 itself? Do you see it as an irrelevance to the main question, or as a further step towards the kind of Community you have always expected?

For me, 1992 underlines a great fallacy by which this whole subject has been haunted in the British debate. It is the fallacy of confusing free trade with a customs union.

1992 is, I think, regarded by many people in the United Kingdom as the achievement of free trade. Now, I have made no secret of the fact that I am, by instinct and prejudice, a free trader – that is to say, I am suspicious of the motives of governments in interfering with the freedom of their citizens to exchange goods and services with the citizens of other countries.

This is what free trade meant in the 19th century. This is the free trade of Cobden and Bright. It is the free trade of Gladstonian England. It is totally compatible, and no other interpretation of free trade *is* compatible, with the ability of a country and of a people to live their own life in their own way, and make their own laws and enjoy national independence. Free trade in *that* sense can exist and can be brought to a high degree of perfection without any requirement for the internal laws of the respective countries to be rendered uniform. Indeed, one of the virtues of free trade is that it facilitates intercourse between those who live under very different systems. It neutralizes, as it were, the consequence for men and women of living under different governments.

It is, in that sense, a profoundly 'liberalizing' external policy for a country to adopt. The subjects of the Grand Turk may live under great oppression, and the Grand Turk may be a very bad monarch: nevertheless, his subjects can enjoy the advantage of exchanging whatever they have that *we* want at a value which is as attractive to them as it is to us.

Now, on the other hand, there is a kind of bad pun about free trade; it is the bad pun that is implicit in the 'E' of the EEC, and it is the bad pun that is lurking over the date 1992. The *other* meaning of free trade is this. Within a country and amongst those who live under the same government and under the same laws, there is, of course, total freedom of trade accompanied by both freedom of movement and all manner of such intercourse as obtains between those who accept the same government and are ready to live under the same laws.

But this is a different meaning of free trade, because it implies that the trade is *only* free if those who participate in it are, in all other respects, similarly conditioned. This interpretation of free trade has quite a long continental European history; and the EEC is not the first time – and 1992 is not the first time – that freedom of trade has been used fallaciously as a means of inculcating the necessity of amalgamation.

After all, the *Zollverein* of 1848 was the basis on which the Prussian Empire was eventually erected, after the dissolution of the Holy Roman Empire; the mediatization, as it is called in Napoleonic terms, of the small Germanic countries of Central Europe was in effect ushered in by their agreement to have a customs union.

Indeed, customs union in itself – the very fact that the word 'Zoll' enters into it, as well as the word 'Verein' (meaning unity) – implies that it involves restriction, albeit a restriction towards the outside world. The Germanic Empire was founded upon *internal* free trade and anything *but* free trade with the rest of the world.

So 1992 to me is pregnant with this trick, this intellectual, or verbal trick, of identifying *Zollverein*, of identifying the theory of the EEC, with what *England* has always meant by freedom of trade.

But if you were prepared to pay the political price, would you agree that Europe as an economic unit — whatever that means — would be stronger by proceeding towards an internal, single market of the kind envisaged by the Community's founding fathers?

I am afraid that I find the words 'strong' and 'strength' repulsive in this context. They conceal a metaphorical, or a quasi-political, assertion that is particularly dangerous to the British given their vulnerability, since the Second World War, to the danger of the 'bullfrog' mentality — namely, to think that what is big, is also powerful. And, incidentally, we need to analyse what we mean by 'power'.

I think some people would argue that they mean the power to enjoy longer holidays, better conditions at work, cleaner environment — having the means to spend money on all the things that most countries want to spend it on.

Welfare?

Yes.

Well, my answer to that is that I accept — I suppose it's simplistic to accept — the welfare theory underlining the freedom of trade; and that is that the wider the freedom to exchange goods and services, the better are the prospects of economic progress and well-being in all the countries whose citizens are allowed that opportunity.

But, of course, there is another aspect to all this — the desire to see the world in terms of 'blocs'. The United States has been very prone to this in its own thinking, and has imposed that thinking upon those that it has taken as its allies. The notion that there is strength — and this has merged into the meaning of *military* strength — in creating an economic bloc; and perhaps the *Zollverein* is waiting in the wings, and the ghost of the German Empire is waiting in the wings, again.

This is not, I must say, a sort of strength in which I wish the United Kingdom to be interested. I don't think we *ought* to be interested. I don't think we ever have as a nation really been interested in the imposition of our will upon others against their will. Now, there are some who would read the history of the British Empire differently from that, but I think there was never a 'will to power' in Britain's external policy, not even in its imperial policy.

And there is a confusion here, between one's ability to use economic resources to impose a political will upon other nations on the one hand; and, on the other hand, the adoption of freedoms which maximize the creation of economic resources.

There is also the fallacy with which we've lived disastrously since the evolution of national income statistics – namely, the international statistical table and the international 'league'. I fear that the use of the word 'competitive' so often in the Prime Minister's mouth, relates to this concept – the notion that there is a league table of output per head, against which one can read off one's success.

But what about the word 'competition' in the mouth of *industry*? I know that industrialists can be notoriously ignorant of politics, but when a businessman says that his business suffers in comparison with his international competitors by virtue of the number of forms has to to fill in, or customs posts he has to pass over, isn't there a sense in which 1992 could help him? Would you object to 1992 if it restricted itself to these kind of matters, or would you say that those are the advantages of a single market that can only be secured by becoming a single nation as well?

I think it's useful in order to clear one's mind on this question to revert to the old distinction between a protective duty and a revenue duty. This is the old meaning of an 'excise'. We impose an excise upon that which is produced both at home and is imported – and we impose the same excise – because the purpose of an excise is not to interfere with trade, it is to raise a revenue.

I would wish to see governments abstaining from forms of taxation, and forms of regulation, of which the object was to interfere with their own citizens' freedom to exchange goods and services with the citizens of other countries. On the other hand, if the Grand Turk likes to put a tax upon currants, then I do not quarrel with the right of the Grand Turk to use that method of raising a revenue in his dominions.

There is another point too which is more important and rather deeper, but which is akin. When people talk about freedom of intercourse, they often slip in 'freedom of movement of *people*'. Now, one of the great virtues of trade is that it is a more efficient substitute for the movement of peoples. We do not need to move into the West Indies in order to enjoy bananas! We enjoy bananas in our northern clime without our having to go to the West Indies, or without the West Indies having to come to enjoy our northern clime. So economically, and in terms of consumption and production, trade is a substitute for the movement of peoples. It's one of the discoveries of advanced economics.

After all, this country is covered with the palaces of bishops who had to move around their dioceses for one reason, in order to enjoy some of the revenues. The medieval king had to travel because only by travelling could he raise and use and exploit a revenue. Now trade has replaced that limitation, and without movement of peoples 'to eat the grass' in another country, we gain all the benefits, without actually moving, of 'eating his grass': we exchange for his grass what we have to offer *him*.

So, it is very important that we don't get into this habit of lumping in with free trade the free movement of persons, which is deeply relevant to the nature of a nation.'

And, indeed, to the single market and 1992. For example, the common acceptance of professional qualifications, such as the law.

I am sure it would be tyrannical for us to attempt to impose, even upon the Germans, the standard which our sixth forms are required to arrive at in the composition of Latin and Greek prose.'

You would, am I right in saying, agree with M. Delors when he asserts that the single market in the way that it is imagined by the EEC, but not by the British government, requires a common currency?

No I don't, because that's what the exchange rate is for. The exchange rate enables citizens of this country and subjects of the

Grand Turk, who has his own currency, to seek nevertheless a common standard of value in the goods and services they exchange.

That's all right for free trade. But if 1992 is about something more than free trade...

Well, it *is* about something more than free trade; it is about something that is being imposed, though they don't understand the full implications of it, upon the people of this country. It is *amalgamation*, and I do not wish to be amalgamated with the Grand Turk.

Quite, but if the *purpose* is amalgamation, then Delors is right in saying that you need a single currency. And so is Lord Cockfield.

Oh yes, this is the illogical argument again from free trade to *Zollverein*. And also, when Delors talks about a 'Europe without frontiers', he means a Europe without *internal* frontiers. He means a Europe that, upon political grounds, will be deciding upon its frontiers with the outside world.

The problem I am attempting to highlight is that we have on the one hand Mrs Thatcher and the British government wanting free trade from 1992...

And so do I.

Oh well then, do you think that it is *possible* to extract free trade from 1992?

Not as the EEC is constituted. The EEC is constituted to use internal free trade as a lever for political unification.

That is the point I was after. And it also means surely that the British government is being hopelessly unrealistic in expecting people like Delors to accept *its* concept of what 1992 ought to be about.

In fact, the proof of all this really lies in the fundamental legislation of 1972. Had the EEC been aiming at free trade in the definition that I have offered, and *not* in the *Zollverein* concept with political intentions, it would not have been necessary for this country, or for any other country – any more than for the parties to EFTA – to abandon their own legislative independence.

People are surprised when they hear me say this, but I think I have at times been unfair to Ted Heath. When Ted Heath in October 1972, after the Royal Assent to the European Communities Act, declared that the objective was economic, monetary, and political union in Europe by 1980 – well, maybe he got his date wrong, but he was nevertheless spelling out the unavoidable implications of what he had induced Parliament to do.

Can we turn specifically to monetary union and the EMS? It is interesting that the Prime Minister's adviser Sir Alan Walters, who has been a stern critic of Britain joining the EMS, nevertheless sees the point in a single currency and economic union. It is also interesting that Nigel Lawson, in his major speech at Chatham House, made a sharp distinction between linking sterling with the Deutsche Mark and a single European currency. He sees the two as unrelated. And one reason why he favours EMS is, like Sam Brittan, that he sees it as an effective discipline against governments inflating.

This is another aspect of the whole question, and it goes back to *stasis* in the Greek City States – the bringing in of the foreigner to help impose your own will upon your own people. I fear that there was an element of this in the persuasion of the Conservative party – and it is an element which hasn't been visible so much in recent years because they now have a majority – to undertake something so 'unnational' as membership of the EEC: the argument that if we go into the EEC we shall have policies imposed upon us that we should like to see and those perishers, our political opponents, don't want.

That is another aspect of seeking a common government. You seek a common government that you believe is more likely to govern in your own class or party interest than a government elected and supported by a majority of your fellow citizens.

I understand that. But looking at it in purely economic terms, what do you say to those who liken the EMS to the old idea of the gold standard?

Well, there are those who regard a government's power to

multiply the currency as a legitimate political instrument; and if my fellow countrymen care to give a majority in Parliament to those who say 'We will give you prosperity through inflation', my answer is that they are perfectly entitled to take that decision – they're making a mistake and they won't get prosperity through inflation, but they have a right to try.

This is where there is an important difference between currency in the modern world and currency through most of human history. Through most of human history, currency has itself been an item of barter. Consequently, no government – not even that of Croesus who put his stamp upon the gold which was dredged out of the river Pactolus – could artificially maintain an unnatural, that is to say a non-market, value of its currency. In modern times, when we have used as money a government promise to pay – when we have invented paper money rather than tradable metals – government has acquired the power to play politics with money; to use its Midas touch – the printing press – as a means of cheating.

Now the right to cheat, and the power to cheat, is essentially an aspect of sovereignty. It's given by the people: they say 'Please cheat us; we want to be cheated; we believe you can benefit us by cheating us, so please cheat and carry on cheating.'

If anybody has expressed the detestation and fear that ought to be attached to the cheating power of government, it is the present Prime Minister. And I think that her instinct against Britain's membership of the EMS has been a right instinct, in that she has understood that a common currency, a currency compulsorily mutually interchangeable, is really to give the power to cheat to someone else.

She's against cheating. She doesn't want the power to cheat to be exercised by the government of the United Kingdom. But *a fortiori* she doesn't want it exercised by somebody else, and she's right.

There is a difference between you and some other opponents of the EEC that is linked to the economic aspects we have been discussing, and also relates to the American dimension that you consider so important. There are some who share your opposition to the EEC, and who don't want the United Kingdom economy to be absorbed into a European state; but neither do they share your dislike of the United States, and certainly not your desire to distance this country from its close economic and defence ties with America. How do you account for this difference?

> I seem to see in what you've posed to me the same underlying misuse of the notion 'economic power' that we discussed earlier. Or alternatively, we are talking about political unification in its aspect of common defence policy, when we are *appearing* to be discussing economics, in which case we are back to the trick of the *Zollverein*.
>
> I remember arguing, and this was before losing the battle over the 1972 Act, that those who were interested in a lasting peace in Europe ought to be aware of the implications of a political unification which included Western Germany.

And indeed a political unification that included a United Germany? The prospect is not so remote as when you first discussed this aspect of the subject. What would that mean to the EEC? If people were to be convinced of your argument concerning the Soviets and the fact that, in your view, they pose no threat to Western Europe, the presence of the Americans in Europe would no longer be regarded as essential. If this encouraged West Germany to attempt to realize *their* dream of reuniting their country . . .

> We're back again pedantically to the old point we have already discussed a great deal, namely the distinction between freedom of trade and *Zollverein* – and *Zollverein* as a basis of political unity. There is no problem at all, much the contrary, in enjoying freedom of trade with a politically reunited North Germany.
>
> But if the EEC is viewed – as I'm sure the Americans wish to view it (which is why they were interested in getting Spain and Greece inside it) as a political, that is a military bloc – then it follows that a reunited Germany which belonged to it would be the most insulting threat that you could imagine to the Soviet Union and would endanger the possibility of a peaceful rearrangement of the pattern of Eastern Europe.
>
> The ambition in military terms of political unity is military unification – the creation of something more solid than an alliance. Alliance you can have, but political unity is an alliance raised to a higher power. The anxiety that must be felt by the Soviet Union

when it looks westwards   is the creation, in alliance with the
United States, of an overwhelmingly powerful military bloc. As
long as North Germany is divided, a West European military bloc
that includes West Germany *only* can be regarded by the Soviet
Union as a manageable antagonist.

I do not believe it *could* regard, or would be right in regarding,
a West European bloc that comprised the whole of the reunited
Northern Germany as something to which a counterpoise could be
arranged without the application of unacceptable duress.

It is because a political unit cannot help but be seen as alliance
– plus – and indeed there is talk about this, that we must bring
common defence policies into the thinking of the European Economic Community – that the possibility is destroyed, or at least endangered, of creating a balance of power in Europe within which
nations have a reasonable prospect of safely developing their own
identities and self government.

One of the sentences I have quoted more than any other out
of the Prime Minister's speech at Bruges was the one in which she
chose to refer to Warsaw, Prague, and Budapest as 'great European
cities.' Warsaw, Prague, and Budapest; Poland, Bohemia, and
Hungary – they cannot, except in a Europe of nations where
there is a balance of power regarded as acceptable by Russia,
develop their nationalities and enjoy freedom of association and
access.'

But returning to Germany. Is it possible, in her desire for reunification, that
Germany might become an ally of those in the EEC who wish to *reduce* the
political nature of the EEC in order to make it appear less of a threat to
Russia? Could the EEC evolve, as a consequence of Germany, into something more acceptable to you?

Well, I can see the argument that if the obstacle to German
reunification is the fear that a reunified Germany within a Western
bloc would necessarily inspire, then a Germany bent upon
reunification is going to wish to reduce the political content of any
association in Western Europe of which it is a part. There's a trade-
off between the two. Indeed, it's rather an attractive thought that
Germany, which has no doubt enjoyed in recent years the spectacle of the British victor chaining itself politically to the nations of

Western Europe, might hold the key to unchaining us. Stranger things than that have happened before.

So let us consider how it all might end. You are still confident that somehow or other, Britain will break free from what she has got herself into ...?

... will recover its legislative and parliamentary independence?

Yes. But do you think this is going to happen through a negotiated withdrawal, and a repeal of Section 2 of the European Communities Act; or do you think it could happen through the development of a two-tier Europe? When one reads the words of people like Lord Cockfield, it is quite obvious that one of the things they fear most is a two-tier Europe with some countries – including Britain – much more loosely associated, outside the EMS, etc. Would *you* see that as a possible escape for politicians scared of losing face, and not wishing to countenance outright withdrawal?

It is the business of politics to achieve movement through one hundred and eighty degrees without loss of face. That's what politicians are trained for – that's their life-long study. No doubt this will be, when the time comes, achieved; but the essential component is that the people of the United Kingdom should clearly enough see the incompatibility of the European Economic Community in the way in which it is developing with what they want to retain. Somewhere along this line there has to be a mutual recognition between the Eurocrats and the British. I use that rather ugly term 'Eurocrats' quite deliberately. I am not sure that our national aspiration to self-government is entirely unshared by some of the other member States of the European Economic Community. So I say there would have to come a moment when there was not a confrontation, but a mutual understanding between Eurocracy and the United Kingdom.

Do you ever worry though that the desire for self-government has left the people of this country? I ask this, because I have been very struck by the number of times you have said in your speeches – virtually every time that a big issue arises – that the British people are at last waking up to what is

going on, and are not going to accept it any longer. But they do accept it. I
think that apart from the EMS, you could argue that the opponents of entry
have lost every fundamental battle. Every time there is a new development,
it is in the wrong direction.

In connection with the EEC?

Yes. It is also significant, is it not, that those people who will be voting for
the first time at the next General Election were born either in or around
1972? That means that the electorate will include people not only with no
memory of the Second World War, but who have never lived under what
you would consider an independent Parliament.

> But it was always a generation which did not remember – or it was
> *very often* a generation which did not remember – those who had
> defended and developed the characteristic constitutional rights of
> the United Kingdom in the past, who have done the same in their
> own time.
>   Perhaps I'm ill-advised in resorting to the metaphor of
> 'reversion to type' – one is in danger of being ill-advised when
> using metaphors taken from sciences with which one is ill ac-
> quainted – but it's like a person whom you recognize at a different
> stage in his life. You say 'that is the same person that I knew as a
> young man'; though every molecule in his body has been changed.
> And yet you say, 'that's the same person. And I know how he is
> going to act. I know how he will behave. At least, I know how *in
> the end* he is going to behave.' It's a strange thing. It's something
> about the nature of human society that you can't talk about it,
> except in anthropomorphic metaphor.

But it might also be said that the young people who are 'reverting to type'
are also more interested in protecting individual freedoms than in discussing from where those freedoms emanate. In other words, if somebody's
freedom is threatened in a way that can only find redress through appeal
to an external authority, that doesn't seem to worry young people very
much.

> You're taking me on to a very big, and possibly not very closely
> related, subject – the question whether what we talk about as

freedom is conditioned, and defined, by the society to which we belong. This raises the whole philosophy of human rights.

But it is relevant for those people who are more interested in the freedom itself than in the way it is enforced – so long as it *is* enforced.

Yes, a right is an enforceable right. There is no meaning in an unenforceable right. So, we are immediately led to ask 'whose force?' Rights depend upon the acceptance of the force that defends them. So, we are referred back again to the concept of society in relation to authority and sovereignty. This is fundamental, philosophically fundamental. Certainly, it's been brought under challenge by the whole system of attempting to codify human rights and make them enforceable. And we've discovered that the defining of human rights is itself an exercise of coercion, as the enforcement is by definition an exercise of coercion.

So, I think that into this aspect of the EEC we're introducing something that is possibly an inheritance from the American and French revolutions – the idea of a freedom detachable from the society in which it is enjoyed. Now, as a Tory, I deny that there is such a thing. For me, rights and freedoms derive from the society to which you belong, are guaranteed by it, and are only desirable because you belong to it.

The EEC is for you still the supreme issue. Why is it, do you think, that the people of this country appear to have accepted membership, albeit without enthusiasm? What went wrong? You genuinely thought in 1972 that the Bill could be defeated. Although you never predicted a victory in the referendum, I think you were surprised by the size of the majority in favour. We have never seen that upsurge of anger and resentment you have always expected and hoped for. So what was it that was lacking? People get the politicians they deserve. And the people could have stopped it.

I don't think the British react very effectively to an abstract threat. You can argue to them that this is the necessary, unavoidable consequence of what they are agreeing to. But they take that very sceptically, until in practical terms it comes home to them. If they are going to say – as some of them say in other contexts, correctly or otherwise – 'Enoch was right' over this too, it will be because the sense of being bound by what they do not want to be bound by has come home to them in practice.

And that may well be beginning to happen. But if it is, why isn't the Labour party grabbing its chance? Is it the Labour party's stupidity – or their reading of national public opinion, which differs from your own – that has led them virtually to drop the issue just when they have an enormous opportunity of being seen to come to the rescue of national sovereignty?

> But then you might have thought that, after the Cruise missiles fiasco, the Labour party had an enormous opportunity to capitalize upon their anti-nuclear stance, which I, as you know, believe to be philosophically and militarily well-founded. Yet they threw it away.

If, then, this is the way that the debate is shaping up, and if there is to be a widespread appreciation of the sovereignty argument, would you be able to entertain the possibility of the Conservative party reverting to type. If so, how far would they have to go to convince you this has happened? Bruges isn't enough, presumably? A helpful sign, perhaps, but Mrs Thatcher is still miles from your position.

> The claims made in that speech for national sovereignty and national parliaments, and the repudiation in that speech of a central overriding authority, come very close to being incompatible with the very nature of the legislation of 1972 and 1986. Of course, incompatible things may be said in the consciousness that they are incompatible and in the intention of living with the incompatibility. But incompatible logically they are; and if deployed in debate in 1972 or 1986, there is no doubt in which direction they would have been regarded as telling.

The above discussion took place in March 1988. Events in succeeding months – including the European elections – are likely to take the debate further. But few would doubt that it is Powell who has articulated in the most compelling and direct fashion the case against Britain's membership of the European Community. It is a case which some are now deploying for themselves. But have they left it too late?

Powell would say that it is never too late. Two significant points that arose from this conversation were the prospect described by Powell of the British people 'reverting to type'; and his acknowledgment of the unwillingness of the British to react to an *abstract* threat.

Only future events will determine to what extent this threat continues to be regarded in abstract terms. If the Prime Minister has decided to fight the European Commission upon the battleground of sovereignty, it will be very difficult for the nation to remain a passive spectator. She occupies the ideal position from which to bring the matter to a head, if that is her intention. It will make her past differences with colleagues seem paltry by comparison. The Conservative party will hardly relish the experience of opening up old wounds.

There are also those who will argue that such blood-letting is unnecessary. Leaving aside whether or not sovereignty is out of date – at least in the sense that it has been traditionally understood – events are now moving so fast that, in the opinion of some, past arguments against Britain's EEC membership, while retaining their interest, are no longer relevant.

This is particularly true of the so-called socialist menace from which the EEC was supposed to rescue all believers in market forces. Now it appears that the debate amongst EEC enthusiasts has turned to the question of whether or not the European Commission should take steps to protect its 'national' industry from international competition. In this context, fear of the Japanese is much more widespread than fear of the red flag. When considering some of the current issues facing the Community – public procurement, Fortress Europe and the like – the real choice is held out to be between either some sort of protected playground or a market prepared to compete on a global scale. The former requires government intervention – but not necessarily socialist in character.

Powell would not be surprised by the turn the argument has taken. His opposition towards protectionism is recorded in this book, and there is no doubt that he remains as much of a free trader as he has ever been. But during the course of the conversation recorded above, Powell also made the point that 'a *Zollverein* is *dirigiste* – a *Zollverein* is making economic law the whole time'. And for Powell, 1992's single market is indeed a *Zollverein*.

If so, it is no wonder that protectionism is again on the agenda. And neither should it ever be forgotten that the Common Agricultural Policy – a protectionist device if ever there was one – is still a principal reason for the European Community's existence.

But then we are brought back to Powell's crucial concern. Nobody would deny that there are valid points on both sides of the political divide which this book has, in part, explored. For Powell, however, an essential test of sovereignty is that these matters should be resolved by the House of Commons. Others say that this approach is no longer tenable; for them, the issues are too interdependent for any single country to have any influence on its own. This returns us to one of the themes of Powell's preface at the beginning of this book. He does *not* believe that the realities of modern business demand political integration; he does not accept that this is the only way of guaranteeing co-operation or a common approach.

Not that Powell is against these two things; as he says in his preface, 'it is but rational, when taking some kind of decisions, to take them to the same effect as other nations'. But, for Powell, these are still decisions to be taken by the nation state. This is a leitmotiv that runs through all his remarks, and it is this that, he contends, will determine in the end whether the European Community pursues its current path, or reverts to some sort of free-trade area. But even if it chooses the former, there is no doubt that Powell still believes that, one day, the British people will demand the recovery of their national sovereignty.

The battle then will be fought out between those who champion Powell's ideal of parliamentary sovereignty, and those who openly, enthusiastically, and with conviction look forward to a single, European State.

Those upon whom it falls to fight the battle will always be indebted to Powell for mapping out the battle-ground; there will at least be no excuse for fighting over 'a little patch of ground that hath in it no profit but the name'.

INDEX